EFFECTIVENESS OF IN-SERVICE TRAINING PROGRAMMES

By

Mrs. Noojilla Rama Subrahmanyam
M.A., M.A. (Litt), M.Ed., M.Phil.
Lecturer in Psychology
District Institute of Educational Technology
Dubacherla
West Godavari District
(Andhra Pradesh)

Editor

Dr. Digumarti Bhaskara Rao
M.Sc., M.A., M.A., M.Ed., Ph.D.
Principal & Professor
R.V.R. College of Education
D-43 (277) S.V.N. Colony
Guntur – 522 006
(Andhra Pradesh)
&
Member, Board of Studies in Education
Acharya Nagarjuna University
e-mail: digumartibhaskararao@rediffmail.com

DISCOVERY PUBLISHING HOUSE PVT. LTD.
NEW DELHI-110 002

Published by:
Tilak Wasan

DISCOVERY PUBLISHING HOUSE PVT. LTD.
4383/4A, Ansari Road, Darya Ganj
New Delhi-110 002 (India)
Phone : +91-11-23279245, 43596064-65
Fax : +91-11-23253475
E-mail : parul.wasan@gmail.com
discoverypublishinghouse@gmail.com
web : www.discoverypublishinggroup.com

***First Edition:* 2012**
ISBN: 978-93-5056-078-5

Effectiveness of In-service Training Programmes

© Digumarti Bhaskara Rao
N.Rama Subhramanyam

All rights reserved. No part of this publication should be reproduced, stored in a retrieval system, or transmitted in any form or by any means: electronic, mechanical, photocopying, recording or otherwise, without the prior written permission of the author and the publisher.

This book has been published in good faith that the material provided by authors is original. Every effort is made to ensure accuracy of material, but the publisher and printer will not be held responsible for any inadvertent error(s). In case of any dispute, all legal matters are to be settled under Delhi jurisdiction only.

Printed at:
Shree Balaji Art Press
Delhi

Dedicated
To

Lord Sri Venkateswara Swamy

Preface

The Right to Education has made the education a fundamental right to the children aged between six and fourteen. With the implementation of RTE, the teaching community has to provide quality education to the students through various modes and means. For this, all the teachers have to undergo in-service training of different kinds to improve their teaching efficiency and the student learning.

The Government of Andhra Pradesh is providing various in-service training programmes to primary school teachers, and among them, the most effective one is Children Learning Acceleration Programme for Sustainability (CLAPS).

The present study is undertaken to study the opinions about the effectiveness of the present in-service training programmes imparted at primary school level. The primary school teachers feel that the present in-service training programmes are very effective and useful.

The State and Central governments should devise effective in-service teacher training programmes to enhance the teaching efficiency of teachers and the learning efficiency of students, and to achieve the goals of universalisation of elementary education and the Right to Education.

Dr. Digumarti Bhaskara Rao
digumartibhaskararao@rediffmail.com
Tele-Mobile: +91 949 3333 555

Contents

1 Introduction

The National Policy on Education (NPE) envisages that free and compulsory education of satisfactory quality should be provided to all children up to the age of 14 years irrespective of caste, creed, sex, religion etc. before we enter the 21st century. The 83rd Constitution Amendment Bill has been introduced to make the right to Elementary Education, a Fundamental right of the child and a fundamental duty of the Government. The target of universalisation of elementary education has been divided into three broad parameters i.e. universal access, universal retention and universal achievement during the Eighth Five Year Plan.

Primary education occupies a significant place in the reconstruction of a developing country like India. It is at this stage the child starts attending a formal school. The National Policy on Education, 1986 emphasizes the importance of giving special attention to quality aspects of primary education. A variety of measures have been proposed by the Union Government for securing participation of girls and boys from the deprived and under-privileged sections of our society.

Universalisation of Elementary Education (UEE) has been the priority area in our educational plan. It is crucial for the development of our nation. Even after sixty years of India's freedom, we have not been able to achieve the desired targets. The attainment of UEE still remains a slogan or a catch word. The reasons for the non-attainment of UEE targets are many and varied such as financial limitations on the part of the Government in allocating substantial funds, lack of commitment and consensus among political parties, illiteracy of parents, poverty, non-availability of educational opportunities and lack of adequate in-service training programmes for working teachers.

It is the responsibility of the Nation to provide Education for All. Education for All means giving quality primary education to all, developing essential skills, competencies and attitudes in all members of society and providing equal opportunities for learning and achievement. It is not sufficient if the child is enrolled in the school, the child should get quality education for which he was admitted in the school.

The Education Commission of 1964-66 greatly emphasized on in-service education of primary teachers. There was need for the organization of a large scale, systematic and coordinated programme of in-service education, so that every teacher would be able to receive at least two or three months of in-service education in every five years of service. The curriculum of these programmes should be planned and organized systematically, materials being developed with great care and the staff in charge being properly oriented.

The document adopted by the World Conference on Education for All (Jomtein, Thailand, 5-9 March, 1990), convened jointly by the Executive Heads of the United Nations Children's Fund (UNICEF), United Nations Development Programme (UNDP), the United Nations Educational, Scientific and Cultural Organization (UNESCO) and the World declared that education is a fundamental right for all people, women and men, of all ages, throughout the world. Some 1500 governments, including policy makers and specialists in education and other major government sectors and 150 non-governmental organizations participated in the Conference.

Even after 60 years of India's freedom, we have not been able to achieve the desired targets. Moreover, the attainment of UEE targets are many and varied, viz., economic constraints on the part of the government in regard to budget allocations, lack of commitment of political parties, poverty, illiteracy of parents, parental ignorance about the need and importance of education, mismatch between the training and placement of teachers at primary level, ineffective supervision, assigning non-academic tasks to teachers, e.g., house listing operations, enumeration, door-to-door survey and mid-day meals and teachers' inability to stay in the villages where they are posted. As a consequence of these, many children initially enrolled in the school do not complete their primary schooling.

Whatever the reason be, our schools failed to attract the children towards schools. Even though we succeeded in enrolling the children in school registers, we were still not able to make them sit in the classroom with joy. Dropout rate of children from schools is very high. The teachers were also confined to the traditional methods of teaching only. The reason for high dropout rate is due to lack of facilities for joyful learning in the schools. In this context there is every need to change the methods of teaching for primary classes and make the teaching more child centered. During the last five decades, there has been a phenomenal increase in the growth of educational facilities at all stages of education. For instance, the number of institutions dealing with the Elementary Education increased. Though the achievements have been substantiated in quantitative terms, but the quality education has not taken place proportionately.

Primary education occupies a significant place in the reconstruction of a developing country. It is at this stage that the child starts attending a formal school. The National Policy on Education, 1986, emphasizes the importance of giving special attention to quality aspects of primary aspects. Several programmes including those on teacher training have been formulated for this purpose. The National Policy on

Education, 1986 gave high priority to UEE. The policy also recognizes that unattractive school environment, unsatisfactory conditions of school building and insufficiency of instructional material function as demotivating factors for children and their parents. Therefore, it laid emphasis on the substantial improvement of primary schools and adequate provision of support services. A variety of measures have been proposed by the Union Government for securing participation of girls and boys from the deprived and underprivileged sections of our society.

A committee under the chairmanship of Mukhi Ram Saikia, Minister of State in MHRD, Government of India, recommended that the Constitution should be amended and "the right to free primary education be made a fundamental right". The recent Right to Free and Compulsory Education Act, August, 2009 has come into force in Andhra Pradesh from April, 2010. This Act works as a weapon in the hands of the child to get quality education.

Various schemes and in-service training programmes have been designed and implemented in most of the States in the country to update teachers' knowledge of content and methodology. Chief among these are OBB, APPEP, SOPT, UEE, Joyful Learning, MLL, DPEP and SSA. Under various schemes and programmes, physical facilities in the schools have been increased; pucca buildings constructed and single teacher schools have been reinforced through posting of additional teachers. In the state of Andhra Pradesh, under different spells of DSC 1990, 1998, 1999, 2000, 2002 and 2006 about 2 lakh additional teachers were recruited to strengthen primary education. Drinking water facilities have been provided by digging bore wells; separate toilets for girls have also been constructed. For the preparation of additional teaching learning material, each school has been sanctioned an amount of Rs. 2000 and each teacher has been sanctioned an amount of Rs. 500.

Although several interventions have been provided for the quality of primary education, a number of studies have revealed that children are not developing with the expected competencies in reading and writing in their mother tongue and also in other subjects at the Primary stage.

Need for qualitative improvement of Primary education, therefore, needs more emphasis on in-service education/ trainings for Primary School teachers periodically. It is one of the significant inputs to improve the quality of primary education. More facilities for in-service education of elementary teachers are needed. The NPE, 1986 envisaged the setting up of DIETs to improve the quality of elementary education and also to attain the goal of Universalisation of Elementary Education. DIETs are responsible for the educational development in their catchment areas, i.e., in the Districts.

One of the functions of DIETs is to provide in-service education for at least 2, 3 weeks duration to all Elementary teachers in the district at least once in five years. This is quite an uphill task if we consider the number of Elementary teachers in the district and the number of Lecturers in DIET who are proposed for the said purpose.

In-service education of teachers working at primary level is the responsibility of DIETs. It is expected that all DIETs should be equipped with full faculty in all their departments and become fully operational. Then only, it would be possible. Each DIET needs to adopt suitable strategies of in-service education in order to cover the target population of teachers within the stipulated frame.

The NPE, 1986 envisaged the setting up of School Complexes all over the country. One of the important functions of school complexes would be to provide professional support to its teachers especially primary school/ upper primary school teachers. Every school complex will have at least one T.V. set and other materials. It is proposed in this context to equip the teachers with the knowledge of professional skills for achieving the competencies fixed by the Department, with the help of SSA. SSA is providing different types of in-service trainings to Primary School Teachers spending huge amounts, utilizing the services of DIET Faculty, Strong Teachers and District Resource Groups. In this connection there is need to study the effectiveness of these training programmes provided to teachers in the improvement of Quality of Primary Education.

In this backdrop the Government has planned and organized several training programmes for teachers of primary classes for quality improvement. Those programmes include OBB, APPEP, SOPT, Joyful learning etc. In 2005-06 a new programme called Children Language Improvement Programme (CLIP) was introduced in primary schools throughout Andhra Pradesh. It aimed at improving the standard of Primary Schools' children in two subjects i.e. Telugu and Mathematics.

The success of CLIP led to another novel programme named Children Learning Acceleration Programme for Sustainability (CLAPS) in the year 2006-07 throughout the state for the improvement of quality of education in primary schools and upper primary schools. This is a statewide programme implemented in all government and aided schools. Subject-wise minimum competencies have been identified in all subjects and focus is laid on achieving these competencies among children. CLAPS is a programme built up on experiences gained in the implementation of Children Language Improvement Programme (CLIP). The children at elementary stage have acquired basic skills in literacy and numeracy due to implementation of CLIP during 2005-06. Now a programme has been taken up to accelerate Children learning in various curricular areas focusing on the expected learning outcomes at every level. Therefore the focus will be in achieving competencies as envisaged across school subjects.

Children Learning Acceleration Programme for Sustainability

CLAPS is designed to achieve subject specific competencies in all curricular areas as given here under:

Languages — Fluency in Reading, Expression and Comprehension, i.e., oral and written and making children as independent readers — developing children's innate abilities like thinking, imagination, creativity in expressing their ideas and developing the logic of analysis, synthesis and evaluation.

Science — Developing the logic of scientific thinking and make children to undertake investigations, explorations and improving the process skills viz., experimentation, observation, problem-solving, discovery, drawing etc.

Mathematics — Developing the logic in solving various arithmetic problems i.e., verbal and oral (mentally) and improving the numerical skills such as problem solving, estimation, prediction, analysis establishing the relationship patterns, framing the rules etc.

Social Studies — To make the child understand society, environment and geography and enhance the child's ability to map.

Teachers were given training for three days on CLAPS for effective motivation and to achieve prescribed competencies among the children in all subjects. DIET and SSA have been conducting a number of training programmes for in-service teachers depending upon the present needs of children and teachers. After the completion of these training programmes, feedback from the teachers who have taken the training is to be taken to know whether the training given has fulfilled its objectives or not. Monitoring teams at different levels assessed the status of implementation and effectiveness of the training programmes.

Effectiveness of training programmes on the job performance of teachers can be evaluated by considering mediating factors which bring out the latent abilities and talents among teachers like creativity, interest in learning new things, commitment and competitiveness, to bring quality among all the students in achieving competencies. CLAPS was introduced in the year 2006-07 and it is being continued in 2007-08 also.

Many training programmes were given during 2007-08 under CLAPS and innovative programmes and also conducted many Melas and Library week celebrations, to bring effective change and also to encourage the teachers to help them in the class room Teaching Learning Process. So, the training given in these areas needs to be implemented in the real classroom situation.

Training Programme on School Complexes

School Complex is a novel and an important concept envisaged by Kothari Commission. Basing on this, about 7000 school complexes have been established. About 10 to 12 primary/upper primary schools come under the purview of a school complex. The lead school headmaster will act as the chairman of that school complex. The purpose of a school complex is to develop the professional competency of teachers. In August, 2007, a one day training was given to teachers on the proper organization of school complex activities. An agenda is suggested and it is to be strictly followed. There is scope for model lessons by senior teachers and discussions on innovative activities that are implemented in the schools. School Complex is conducted once in a month.

Training Programme on Computer Aided Learning (CAL)

Government has supplied computers to some schools having electricity facility. A number of CDs have been developed for this purpose. Those CDs are directly or indirectly related to the syllabus for I to VII classes. In order to use the CDs in a proper manner, training was given to the teachers having CAL. Pre-activity before displaying the CD, post-activity after displaying the CD, etc., are discussed in this programme. A feedback proforma is also developed which is to be filled in by the teachers and to be submitted to the authorities.

Training Programme on 'Vindam–Nerchukondam'

Government is spending huge investment for broadcasting Radio lessons for primary classes. The class teacher has to take the responsibility for successful implementation of this programme. Training programme is given to teachers on the organization of the radio lesson. Pre activity, actual radio lesson and post activity are the three important aspects to be observed effectively. Feedback of the teachers as well as pupils is taken on the effectiveness of the lesson.

Training Programme to Vidya Volunteers

Every year SSA is appointing vidya volunteers in the place of vacancies of regular teacher posts. Many of these vidya volunteers are trained and in some cases untrained graduates have also been appointed due to non-availability of trained candidates. SSA has arranged training programme to these people also on effective class room transaction. In 2007-08, about 2300 vidya volunteers have been recruited and all of them have been given 5 days training.

Learning Enhancement Programme

Recently the government has introduced this Learning Enhancement Programme with slight modifications in CLAPS. All the necessary competencies have been included so as to be useful for 'A' grade students. This is a comprehensive quality programme being implemented to address quality in a holistic and sustainable way. The focus of L.E.P. is to enhance children achievement in basic competencies in all subject areas from class I to V, meaningful engagement of children in learning programme and appropriate professional support to the teachers for improved classroom processes. The following are the major component of L.E.P.

- Achievement of class specific, subject specific essential learning competencies.
- Improved Teaching learning process — 100 per cent utilization of time and engagement of children — time on task.
- Improved awareness procedures which are competency specific — oral, written and performance.
- Performance Indicators — Teachers, Head Teachers, MEOs and other functionaries or system level making them accountable with the clarity.
- Improved participating parents in school matters.

Necessary material, modules have been developed on the L.E.P. as above and adequate training was provided to all the teachers and field functionaries to implement the programme.

After conducting so many training programmes for teachers, assessment and evaluation of these programmes is necessary. The present study was taken up to find out the effectiveness of training programmes on the professional performance of in-service teachers. This study collects the general information of teachers on the trainings received, the status of implementing the planned curriculum and performance in the classroom, feedback from the teachers and also suggestions on the Training Programmes.

John Herbert believes that Training for teachers can only mould the teacher to transact the Teaching Learning Processes to mould the child. V.S. Jha stressed on the role of the Training to teachers in making the child into a man. Dr. Dart of California, University opines that teacher has to update his skills by adopting the latest strategies in Teaching.

In this background the present study has been taken up to know the effectiveness of In-service Training Programmes imparting at primary school level.

STATEMENT OF THE PROBLEM

A Study of the Effectiveness of In-service Training Programmes Imparting at Primary School Level.

NEED FOR THE STUDY

The main aim of imparting education to the people is 'all must learn' and 'all must prosper'. For providing education of satisfactory quality at elementary stage, several interventions were launched in the last few years by Sarva Siksha Abhiyan. The major emphasis focussed to achieve quality education among primary school children is imparting training programmes to in-service teachers. Kothari Commission has recommended for at least 2 weeks of in-service training programmes to teachers on the emerging new trends. Unless the teachers are given proper training on the latest methodologies, they cannot implement it in the classroom.

Whenever the government is introducing new quality initiatives, the teachers are being given training to implement the new interventions in schools. During the year 2003–04, Quality Improvement Programme (QIP) was implemented with a clearly articulated objective that all children should achieve minimum specified competency levels in the 3 R's (Reading, Writing and Arithmetic) within 45 days of intensive teaching in mission mode. This programme attempted to build the capacities of teachers with extra emphasis on child development. As an improvement over this intervention, during the year 2005-06, Sarva Siksha Abhiyan, Andhra Pradesh has introduced a novel quality improvement programme in the name of Children's Language Improvement Programme (CLIP).

For up-scaling this quality improvement program and also to achieve the set objective of making all children read, write and do arithmetic operations, the Children Learning Acceleration Programme for Sustainability (CLAPS) was introduced during the year 2006-07. In order to achieve the competencies among the children, all the teachers in the State were given three days training. Also trainings were conducted on school complex activities, Vindam–Nerchukundam, computer aided learning, etc.

The main objective of CLAPS is to attain minimum competencies among children. By implementing, it is expected that some changes might come such as improvement in the attendance of children, attention on 'B' group children etc. For this, fixation of classroom responsibility on teachers, implementing innovative programmes such as wall paper, school post box etc and strengthening of monitoring of schools by DIET faculty, school complex headmasters, Mandal Educational Officers etc. have been stressed.

Unless there is an assessment or evaluation on the training programmes conducted, no feedback from teachers is possible for further planning. As the teachers are the actual target group in the entire system of education, their views and feelings are very much necessary. Conducting training programmes in an effective manner will yield the desired result. Now a time has come to make an assessment on the effectiveness of these training programmes given to primary schools' teachers and also to see the achievement levels of the children after implementation of the CLAPS and other training programmes in class rooms. Also to see whether there is any effectiveness of these programmes and how the teachers are responding towards these training programmes. By getting feedback from teachers on the effectiveness of these training programmes, further plan of action is possible. Hence the present study "A Study of the Effectiveness of In- service Training Programmes Imparting at Primary School Level.

SCOPE OF THE STUDY

The present study is confined to West Godavari District of Andhra Pradesh. The sample selected for the study was in-service teachers of primary schools working in Urban, Rural and Tribal areas. The size of the sample of the present study is 150 teachers, taking 50 from each area. Two mandals were selected from each area. 10 to 12 schools have been randomly selected for this purpose.

The variables chosen for the study are gender (male and female), locality (urban, rural and tribal areas), educational qualifications (Degree or below and P.G.) and experience (15 or more years and less than 15 years).

OBJECTIVES OF THE STUDY

The following objectives are framed for the present study:

1. To find out the attitude of primary teachers towards the effectiveness of in-service training programmes.
2. To find out the difference in the attitude of male and female primary teachers towards the effectiveness of in-service training programmes.
3. To find out the difference in the attitude of urban and rural primary teachers towards the effectiveness of in-service training programmes.
4. To find out the difference in the attitude of urban and tribal primary teachers towards the effectiveness of in-service training programmes.
5. To find out the difference in the attitude of rural and tribal primary teachers towards the effectiveness of in-service training programmes.
6. To find out the difference in the attitude of graduate (or intermediate) and post-graduate primary teachers towards the effectiveness of in-service training programmes.
7. To find out the difference in the attitude of more experienced (15 or more years of teaching experience) and less experienced primary teachers (less than 15 years of teaching experience) towards the effectiveness of in-service training programmes.

EDUCATIONAL IMPLICATIONS

Most of the teachers might have positive attitude and high inclination towards in-service training programmes as these programmes will enrich their professional growth and skills. Also by knowing the type of conducting the training programme, the department can plan for the betterment of the inputs, improvement of infrastructural facilities etc. Also it is very important to know the attitude of teachers towards these training programmes because they are the implementing people in class room situation. By knowing the attitude of the teachers, the government can plan for the suitable training programmes so as to develop positive attitude among them. By knowing the feedback from the teachers on the facilities provided, resourcefulness of the resource persons, the type of programmes suitable for implementation, the department can plan accordingly. By providing training on the latest methodologies, joyful teaching and learning environment will take place in the class rooms. Hence this study will be helpful for future planning of in-service training programmes.

2 Review of Related Literature

Review of earlier related research literature, relevant documents and media reports help the investigator namely:

(a) in concept clarification;

(b) in avoiding redundancy of research efforts;

(c) in making decisions about methods and tools of research;

(d) in identifying gaps in the knowledge related to the area and of the present work; and

(e) in formulating objectives and hypothesis of the study.

The uses of the review of research mentioned by Best (1988) and Key (1987) have been highlighted by several other authors of textbooks on research methodology.

Every piece of ongoing research needs to be connected with the work already done, to attain an overall relevance and purpose. The review of literature thus becomes a link between the research proposed and the studies already done. It tells the reader about aspects that have been already established or concluded by other authors, and also gives a chance to the reader to appreciate the evidence that has already been collected by previous research, and thus projects the current research work in the proper perspective.

A large part of review of literature actually needs to be done even before the research project is formalized. This is essential to make sure that you are not repeating the work that someone has already done earlier. Sometimes, if the research proposed by you has already been undertaken earlier, then it provides you an option of modifying your work by adding a new perspective or altering some of the methods of research to obtain a perspective that will be different from earlier works and thus more valuable. Occasionally, your work may be exact repetition of the work done earlier, but with a different set of data or sources of facts, and purpose of the research may just be seen if your results are similar to earlier works or otherwise.

A good researcher usually goes through a lot more literature than is actually incorporated in the paper. This is because different literature may have differing relevance for the current project and all of it may not worth reporting in the end, but in the initial phase, when you are looking for all aspects of an issue that could be relevant one would like to extensively explore the literature and see if any relevant findings are already available. Some of the literature reviewed is directly relevant and hence used as a preface to explain the background of work. Then other reports may be relevant from the point of view of the project as they provide some clues to the puzzle by suggesting a hypothesis, which may be the subject matter of your research project.

Lastly, review of literature is also important to highlight difference in opinions, contradictory findings or evidence, and the different explanations given for their conclusions and differences by different authors. In some cases, an analysis of these factors can help one understand may facets of a complex issue and at other times, such analysis can lead to a new possibility that can be researched upon in the current project. Thus review of literature is a very important part of one's research.

To summarize, there is hardly any research project which is totally unrelated with research that has already taken place. Usually every individual research project only adds to the plethora of evidence on a particular issue. Unless the existing work, conclusions and controversies are properly brought about, most research work would not appear relevant, nor will it appear important in the whole framework. Thus, review of literature is a very important aspect of any research both for planning your work as well as to show its relevance. Review of related literature provides theories, ideas and explanations of a new problem. It suggests methods, procedures, sources of data and statistical techniques appropriate to the solution of the problem. It helps to sharpen and define understanding of existing knowledge of the problem area and provides a background for the research project. It also helps the researcher not only in providing information available in the field of research but in suggesting the methods to be adopted, avoiding the mistakes done by others and in locating misconceptions in the earlier discoveries by others.

Review of literature, thus, helps the researcher in the identification of the problem, in the selection of methods, tools and data analysis techniques and also in guarding against the likely pit falls in the process of research. The researcher stands to gain from the experiences of other early researches in the field and gets guidance from them. He/she collects all possible solutions to the problem under study, all possible ways of interpreting the phenomenon being studied or all possible ways of understanding the true nature of the knowledge being discovered. From all the possibilities so collected, the researcher will select a feasible one to try out.

Research takes the advantage of the knowledge which has accumulated in the past as a result of constant human endeavours. Any worthwhile research in any field of knowledge requires an adequate familiarity with the work which has been done already in the same area. A summary of the writings of recognized authorities and of previous research provides sufficient evidence that the research is familiar with what is already known and what is still unknown. Since the effective research is based upon previous knowledge, this step helps to eliminate the duplication of what has been already done besides helping in fixation of useful objectives, formation of appropriate hypotheses, drawing of meaningful conclusions, and making commendable suggestions. (*Bhaskara Rao, D.*, 1989).

Citing studies that show substantial agreement and those that seem to present conflicting conclusions help to sharpen and define understanding of existing knowledge in the problem area, provide a background for the research project and make the reader aware of the status of the issue. Parading a long list of annotated studies relating to the problem is ineffective and inappropriate, only those studies that are plainly relevant, competently executed and clearly reported should be included in the review of related literature (*Bhaskara Rao, D*. 1997).

The review of literature becomes a link between the research proposed and the studies already done. It tells the reader about aspects that have been already established or concluded by other authors, and also gives a chance to the reader to appreciate the evidence that has already been collected by previous research, and thus projects the current research work in the proper perspective.

A brief review of the previous investigations pertaining to the present study is very essential as it gives the present investigator an understanding of the previous works that have been done and also enables the investigator to know the means of getting to the frontier in the field of study. Unless it is learnt what others have done and what still remains to be done, the present investigator cannot develop a research project that would contribute to furthering knowledge in the field.

THEORETICAL PERSPECTIVES

Theoretical information provides the information related to the in-service training programmes that are imparted at primary school level I Andhra Pradesh.

In-service Education of Teachers

School quality particularly at the primary level is low. This is a matter of serious concern. There is widespread agreement that the achievement of successful schooling is crucially dependent on the quality of teaching workforce. (Husen et al, 2003). Teacher education — both pre-service and in-service is responsible for developing quality teaching work-force. It is generally observed that the quality of pre-service teacher education is low. It does not equip prospective teachers with requisite knowledge, skills and attitudes to perform effectively in their work-situation. "In-service education of teachers is considered to be key aspect of school improvement efforts." (*Sparks and Loucks — Horsley*, 1990)

The training, retraining and updating of practicing teachers are widely recognized as essential factors in the development of teachers' quality. Teacher quality is a major, perhaps the major factor, contributing to improvement in learning outcomes of students (*Husen et.al*, 2003). Prior to 1986, in-service education of teachers was a sporadic affair. The National Policy on Education (NPE) (1986) laid a great deal of emphasis on in-service education of teachers on a continuing basis to improve school quality and thereby to achieve Universal Primary Education (UPE) and Universal Elementary Education (UEE). Enormous resources-human and material are being invested into in-service education of teachers. Presently every teacher is being imparted in-service education for 20 days in a year under Sarva Siksha Abhiyan — the flagship programme of the Government of India.

Though in-service education programmes for teachers are being organized on a continuing basis, but very little is known about the effectiveness of these programmes. Very little information is available whether the training experiences have improved classroom processes of teachers. There are studies which reveal that pupils' achievement only increases when teachers present appropriate content in effective ways in the classroom. "Teachers attending in-service courses often complain that in-service courses are too theoretical, and are too far removed from their daily working experiences. Training activities therefore, do not result in improvement in teachers' instructional behaviours' (*Van Tulder*, 1992). Bolam (1987) too reported that "information imparted to teachers is insufficiently related to the specific needs and concerns of the participants. They tend to offer theory which is unrelated to practice. They tend to over-use lecture and discussion methods. In consequence, they are ineffective in influencing teacher performance and school improvement". It can be effective only if it is based on the entry level capabilities of teachers. "A look into the effectiveness of contemporary staff development literature reveals that teachers learn little from traditional in-service training workshops (*Smylie, Mark* and *Miretzky, Debra* (Eds.)(2004)".

The Education Commission of 1964-66 greatly emphasized on in-service education of primary teachers. There was need for the organization of a large scale, systematic and coordinated programme of in-service education, so that every teacher would be able to receive at least two or three months of in-service education in every five years of service. The curriculum of these programmes should be planned and organized systematically, materials being developed with great care and the staff in charge being properly oriented.

Best Practices for In-service Training Programmes

Korinek, Schmid, and McAdams (1985) examined the literature to identify the most commonly stated guidelines for producing effective in-service programmes. The review led to reports in the literature that met four criteria:

(a) involved work that was conducted in the United States;

(b) published after 1957;

(c) included specific recommendations and/or conclusions about in-service for practicing teachers; and

(d) published in a refereed journal if a comparison or test of procedures was described.

From over 100 reports, only 17 studies met the criteria. 'Best practice' statements were derived from tallying the number of times a specific practice was mentioned in the reports. If a specific practice was mentioned six or more times, it was considered a best practice. The best practices were associated with the three most common models of in-service programmes: information transmission, skill acquisition, and behaviour change.

The following 14 best practices emerged:

- Effective in-service is usually school-based rather than college-based (skill acquisition, behaviour change).
- Administrators should be involved with the training and fully support it (information transmission, skill acquisition, behaviour change).
- In-service activity should be offered at convenient times for participants (information transmission, skill acquisition, behaviour change).
- In-service should be voluntary rather than mandatory (information transmission).
- Rewards and reinforcement should be an integral part of an in-service programme (information transmission, skill acquisition, behaviour change).
- In-service programmes should be planned in response to assessed needs (information transmission, skill acquisition, behaviour change).

- Activities which are a general effort of the school are more effective than 'single shot' presentations (skill acquisition, behaviour change).
- Participants should help plan the goals and activities of the in-service training (skill acquisition, behaviour change).
- Goals and objectives should be clear and specific (information transmission, skill acquisition, behaviour change).
- In-service activity should be directed at changing teacher behaviour rather than student behaviour (behaviour change).
- Individualized programmes are usually more effective than those using the same activities for the entire group (skill acquisition, behaviour change).
- Participants should be able to relate learning to their back home situations (information transmission, skill acquisition, behaviour change).
- Demonstration, supervised practice, and feedback are more effective than having teachers store ideas for future use (skill acquisition, behaviour change).
- Evaluation should be built into in-service activity (information transmission, skill acquisition, behaviour change). (*Korinek et. al.*, 1985, p. 35)

According to Locke (1985), in-service programmes are most effective when teachers are heavily involved in the planning process. Wood, McQuarrie, and Thompson's (1982) research-based model advocates involving participants in planning training programmes. Participants serve on planning teams which assess needs, explore various research-based approaches, select content, determine goals and objectives, schedule training sessions, and monitor implementation of the programme.

In-service programmes are likely to be successful to the degree that the instructors are effective communicators, are or have been teachers themselves, and are able to model the skills they are teaching others (Vacca, 1983). In reviewing the research, Wood and Kleine (1987) found that teachers prefer their peers as trainers. Wu's (1987) review of the research found that when peers are trainers, teachers feel more comfortable exchanging ideas, play a more active role in workshops, and report they receive more practical suggestions. However, there is evidence that expert trainers who have the critical qualities teachers value in their peers can also be highly effective (*Crandall*, 1983).

Some studies have been conducted on the effectiveness of training programmes in India and abroad with different objectives in mind. Not only individual researchers but also organizations like SSA, NCERT have also conducted some research studies on in- serving programmes.

In-service Training Programmes and Teaching Methodologies

Participatory: Participatory methods of teaching and learning are characteristic of several teacher training programmes. In Bangladesh, for example, sub-cluster training sessions rely heavily on the teacher trainees' active involvement in the demonstration lessons, training modules, co-curricular activities and open discussions with parents and school managing committee members. In China, participatory methods are utilized in training activities both within and outside teacher training schools. These include experience sharing, group discussions and summarizing successful experiences. Essential to the conduct of Indonesia's radio in-service training are learning group activities.

Reflection-Action-Reflection: In Brazil, teachers bring their practices, questions and needs to the SMEC, where these topics are discussed and reflected upon, backed by UNIJUI teachers. Later, the primary teachers discussed about the board meeting and decide on new sets of action to be performed. This back and forth process allows them to experimentally design their grade curriculum, set up goals and define basic concepts to be explored in each content area.

Multiple Interactions: India's CIG programme requires that the trainees have a variety of interactions with self-learning materials, with audio-visual materials, with their evaluators, with counselors, teachers and peers during contact programmes. The participants in Egypt's upgrading programme have the same types of interactions, with the exception of interaction with counsellor.

Micro-teaching: Micro-teaching method, which focuses on one specific teaching competency at a time, is an essential feature of Pakistan's PTOC handled by AIOU. It is also one of the learning-by-doing. Methods used by China's teacher training schools.

Peer Coaching: Peer coaching/training is the hallmark of Nigeria's PISA. 'Expert' teachers serve as role models and trainers for their peers. It is also done by China's key teachers.

In-service Training Programmes—Teacher Education Models

The programmes can also be classified according to the teacher education models they represent. Ellis (1987) identified these forms: formal award courses, non-award activities, and school-based activities.

Formal Award Courses: These are courses offered by universities and colleges and "include conversion courses for the purpose of upgrading qualifications, a wide variety of specialist graduate diplomas, the in-service B.Ed. degree and Masters' degree in education" (*Ellis*, 1987, p.63). Programmes offering such courses are those of Egypt (B.A. or B.Sc.), India (CIG) and Indonesia (credits).

Non-award Activities: This category refers to " short-term courses, seminars, conferences and other activities organized by employing authorities, tertiary institutions, teachers' subject associations and other individuals and groups"(Ellis,1987, p.63). Examples of these are the cases of Mexico and Pakistan.

School-based Activities: These are made up of "seminars, workshops, project activities and the like arranged at the school level". Included in this type are the training activities conducted in Bangladesh, Brazil and China.

In-service Training Programmes and Outcomes

The results of the programmes generally support the well established power of training to modify the knowledge, instruction skills and attitudes of teachers (*Sparks* and *Loucks — Horsley*).

Awareness of knowledge: The stated aims of the in-service training programmes of Egypt, India and Mexico reflect the desired cognitive outcomes. Reports indicate that the teachers, indeed, gained knowledge of new trends in their academic specializations and education(Egypt); gained understanding of concepts, problems and processes relating to guidance of elementary school children (India) ; were oriented to technique-practice topics in the teaching-learning process (Mexico).

Skill Development: China reports the successful attainments of basic teaching skills by trainees in several provinces. Egypt's programme resulted in upgrading the professional level of participants. Several studies reveal that the major goal of Pakistan's programme namely, improving the teachers' practical skills (e.g., presenting, blackboard work, responding) has been achieved.

Attitude Change: Enhancement of teachers' self confidence in Brazil was attained through SMEC-UNIJUE's emphasis on their ability to write text books and develop self-learning, teaching materials. Mexico however was concerned about teachers' attitude change vis-à-vis teaching-learning process, teaching practice and school-community relationship.

Transfer of Training and Executive Control: This desired outcome pertains to 'the appropriate and consistent use of new strategies in the class room. Success in this regard is reported by Bangladesh, with an increased use of teaching aids in the class room. In China, class room observations and interviews with principals provide vivid examples of the teachers' progress and achievement in teaching after their training. A research study undertaken in Pakistan (*Nighat*, 1966) shows that effectiveness of the training programme as found in the class room performance of training graduates.

In-service Training Programmes — Issues and Problems

Training of Trainers: Poorly trained trainers are a major problem in Bangladesh. Their lack of training results in weak supervision and monitoring of sub-cluster training. A similar concern for the quality of trainers also been raised by China.

Administration: In-sufficient administrative autonomy of the schools and autocratic municipal administrative structure are problems for Brazil. Smooth functioning of the programme is affected by lack of control over the budget and the rather centralized planning, despite the appearance of decentralization. Mexico, on the other hand experiences a lack of continuity in institutional support.

Finances, facilities and resources: Although many countries allotted special funds for in-service teacher training, many teacher training schools are experiencing financial difficulties with respect to their new training tasks. A related concern, as cited in a survey conducted in Egypt, is that of high tuition fees. Other problems reported are shortage of facilities and delay in the distribution of text to the participants.

Motivation: The growing neglect of regulations governing the training programme of Egypt seems to indicate a gradual decline in motivation for work and study among participants, university staff members and administrators. The lack of 'customer friendly' study centers in India that are free of formalities, procedure-orientedness and bureaucracy, seems to dampen the spirit of learning of the parents who are like the teachers, participants.

In-service Training Programmes and Innovative Features

The most significant feature of the in-service teacher training Programme of India is its focus on child's holistic development. By training teachers and parents in matters relating to guidance of the elementary school child, the programme gives due attention to an often neglected but essential area in education. The assumption underlying this decision is that when primary schools teachers and parents properly understand the needs of the children, they will under take actions that may promote the children's retention in schools and facilitate their academic achievement. The involvement of parents in this programme is another novelty in itself. It clearly communicates the message that at the primary level the children's cognitive, affective and psycho motor domains are a joint responsibility of teachers and parents. Finally, the programme uses the collaborative project strategy, bringing together the strengths and resources of two institutions, the NCERT and IGNOU. The strategy makes possible another innovation, that of using distance education for training in guidance and counselling.

Salient Features of the Guidelines for In-Service Teacher Training

NCERT has revised the guidelines for annual in-service training in the form of 'The Reflective Teacher'. The Key features of the guidelines developed by NCERT are:

1. It takes into account the 'Constructivist' approach, as advocated in NCF 2005. This means that the teacher should act as a 'facilitator', and should work towards creating a variety of learning experiences in and out of the classroom that enable children to construct knowledge from activities and experiences in day to

day life. The teacher is not to be a 'transmitter' of knowledge to passive recipients (the children).

2. This approach requires teachers to be reflective, that is they need to become 'mindful enquirers' into their own experiences, to guide children meaningfully.
3. The guidelines advocate a 'split up' model of in service training, in which 6-8 days training is provided at the BRC/DIET level and 2 days training through actual observation of classroom situations. Thereafter, teachers are expected to return to their school settings for 2-3 months, to try out the recommended methodologies and ideas. At the end of the training programme, they once again return to the BRC/DIET for 2 days to share their experience and reflect on the new ideas before they complete the training.
4. The guidelines recommend a formal training duration of 10 days, as evident from above.
5. In keeping with NCF 2005, the guidelines recommend training of teachers in areas such as art and heritage crafts, health and physical education, work education and education for peace, besides training in basic subjects like language, EVS and Mathematics.
6. The guidelines stress identification of training needs and development of appropriate training modules through BRGs/DRGs/SRGs. It is also recommended that the training design should emphasize local contextuality and specificities in the teaching learning situation.
7. A list of suggested readings, educational audio and video programmes for teachers have also been provided in the guidelines.

CLAPS — Competencies

Telugu	:	Fluent Reading and Reading Comprehension Self Expression through Writing

Hindi : Listening and Speaking

English : Fluent Reading and Speaking

Mathematics : Oral and Mental Mathematics

Problem Solving (Written Problems)

Social Studies : Conceptual understanding and Mapping Skills

Science : Conceptual Understanding and Experiments/Drawing

CLAPS focuses on ways of learning and the very processes involved in the development of various subject specific competencies among the children. The programme focuses on the capacity building of teachers along with on job support. Appropriate literature, teaching learning material has been provided to teachers and students.

Improved field monitoring and on job support, regular feedback and take up regular reviews. Monthly feedback through review at School, Mandal, District and State Level.

CLAPS — Practical Orientation Programme

The programme emphasis on minimum quality processes which are subjected specific in Classroom Transaction.

Formulating subject-wise competencies to be acquired by the children and ensuring for the attainment by all children.

Specific subject-wise programmes/clubs i.e., Science Clubs, Language Club, Maths Club etc., through pupil participation.

Projects as a major mode of transaction of curriculum.

Monitoring

Monitoring was planned at 5 levels, viz.,

School Level Monitoring: Regular monitoring by the School Head Master – Weekly review of performance of teachers and children.

Cluster Level: The Headmaster of School Complex (CRC) shall monitor the schools of the cluster on regular basis and conduct performance reviews.

Mandal Level Monitoring: Monitoring by Mandal Education Officer and Mandal Resource Persons. External assessment of pupils' progress by MRPs and awarding the grades to class/school.

District Level Monitoring: Monitoring teams have been constituted with Deputy Educational officers, DIET Faculty, Selected HMs and School Assistants of High Schools

Academic Monitoring of Schools by DIET Faculty

Distribution of mandals among the DIET staff who monitors the schools and review the performance at MRC level.

State level monitoring: Review of performance of schools, by the State Level Resource Group and Sectoral officers of SSA along with State Project Director.

Reviews

School level review with the teachers on every Saturday from 3.30 to4.30 p.m. by HM.

Mandal level review with MRPs & HM once in a month by MEO.

District level review with divisional monitoring teams and MEOs once in a month by D.E.O. & A.P.C.

State level review with district observers, DEOs and APCs once in a month by SPD.

Strengths

62 per cent Pupil performance in basic Language and Arithmetic Competencies at primary level under CLIP

- Reading — 68.61 per cent
- Writing — 57.83 per cent

- Addition — 76.44 per cent
- Subtraction — 71.99 per cent
- Multiplication — 54.10 per cent
- Division — 43.19 per cent

The following general objectives are formulated to achieve quality among children.

(i) Special strategies for 1st and 2nd classes

(ii) Focus on pupils' attendance and discussion with parents on this aspect.

(iii) To assess the achievement level of pupils periodically and achieving the set objectives through good monitoring.

(iv) To fix up responsibility on all the officers of the department including teachers.

(v) To equip the Headmaster of the school as the first monitoring officer of the school.

The specific objectives of CLAPS are:

1. At least 80 per cent of the schools should be in 'A' grade.
2. To fix up class-wise responsibility to teachers.
3. Pupils' present should be at least 90 per cent of enrolment.
4. Teachers should be in schools in school timings. No other work should be entrusted to them.

Class-wise and Subject-wise Competencies

For 1st class the following competencies are fixed:

Telugu: Action songs, speaking, reading and writing.

Mathematics: Counting, Ascending and descending order, Addition, subtraction and oral maths.

For 2nd class the same competencies are set for Telugu.

For Mathematics Number concept, Addition, Subtraction, Multiplication and division and oral maths.

For classes 3rd, 4th and 5th the following competencies are set:

Telugu: Understanding the text (Reading and understanding the read items), Sweeya Rachana (Writing on their own)

Mathematics: Mental arithmetic and writing mathematics

English: Speaking and Reading

Environmental Science – 1: Mapping skills and Conceptual understanding

Environmental Science – 2: Field experiments and Conceptual understanding.

Special strategies for 1st and 2nd classes:

1. Fixing up responsibility of 1st and 2nd classes to regular teachers.
2. Implementing Readiness programme in the first two months.
3. Adoption of joyful learning strategies.
4. To make use of running black board.
5. Action songs, songs, stories, drawing pictures etc. to be made part and parcel of teaching learning process.
6. To call the children with their names.
7. To prepare Annual Action Plan.
8. At least 80 per cent of the children should do the activities in a lesson. Only then the teacher should go to the next lesson.
9. Conducting review meetings regularly with teachers and extending co-operation to them.
10. Discussions in school complex meetings and attaining quality.

Action Plan for Conducting CLAPS

1. Conducting base line test in the month of July and dividing the children into A and B groups basing on the levels of the children. 'A' group children are those who possess the requisite level in competencies of their standard and 'B' group children are those who do not possess the requisite competencies.
2. To record month-wise progress of the children individually.
3. To achieve quality, the following steps have to be taken:
   (*a*) fixing up class-wise responsibilities to teachers;
   (*b*) Monitoring by Headmaster of the school;
   (*c*) Headmaster's review meetings with teachers on 1st and 3rd Saturdays;
   (*d*) To conduct parents' meeting every month;
   (*e*) To visit the houses of children who are absent for 3 days or more;
   (*f*) Effective monitoring by mandal level to state level teams;
   (*g*) Regular teacher for 1st class;
   (*h*) To appoint vidya volunteers as per requirement;
   (*i*) To see that Instructional time is totally utilized
   (*j*) Special strategies for *A* and *B* groups of children;
   (*k*) Library hour to be set up in the time table and book reading to be made compulsory.
4. To make DIETs active participants in the programme and DIET lecturers to be given mandal-wise responsibilities.
5. Teachers to complete their regular syllabus as usual and achieve the desired competencies among the children.
6. Question papers to be prepared by the teachers for their class on their own.

7. To involve the school complex headmaster in schools' monitoring.
8. Review the progress of the schools mandal wise, district-wise and state-wise and to take further steps accordingly.

Training Programme on Vindam-Nerchukundam Radio Programme

This training programme emphasizes on the proper implementation of radio lessons that are to be broadcasted regularly for some class of primary section. In this training programme, emphasis is given on pre-activities to be conducted before the children actually listen to the radio programme. The other points stressed are how should be the seating arrangement of the class at the time of this programme. What is the role of the teacher and the children while the lesson is going on. What is the feedback of children on these programmes, how to record them and what the post activities are? Modules wee supplied duly noting the day-wise time table of lessons.

Learning Enhancement Programme (LEP)

Quality is one of the most important parameter of SSA. In almost all the activities under the Programme under various interventions it is given its own priority. A.P. SSA launched a new scheme under the title 'Learning Enhancement Programme' and providing to schools. This is a comprehensive quality programme being implemented to address quality in a holistic and sustainable way. The focus of L.E.P. is to enhance children achievement in basic competencies in all subject areas from class I to V, meaningful engagement of children in learning programme and appropriate professional support to the teachers for improved classroom processes. The following are the major component of L.E.P.

- Achievement of class specific, subject specific essential learning competencies.

- Improved Teaching learning process — 100 per cent. utilization of time and engagement of children — time on task.
- Improved awareness procedures which are competency specific — oral, written and performance.
- Performance Indicators — Teachers, Head Teachers, MEOs and other functionaries or system level making them accountable with the clarity.
- Improved participating parents in school matters.

Necessary material, modules have been developed on the L.E.P. as above and adequate training was provided to all the teachers and field functionaries to implement the programme.

Under L.E.P. grade specific and subject specific competencies have been identified and is being followed for providing competency specific learning process and undertaking competency based pupil assessment procedures. The children performance is being graded under each competency under 'A', 'B', 'C'. 'A' denotes performance of the competencies up to the mark by this child. 'B' denotes average performance and the children may turn to 'A' with appropriate parent/teacher support. The 'C' grade denotes no performance of the child against the competencies. The 'C' grade children required more teacher support to improve their performance. The teachers undertaking assessment based on teacher made test items which are competency based and children performance is required under A, B, C categories. Based on above benefits the children are being provided with special support/remedial teaching. Schools are being graded with A, B, C, D based on children performance. This was implemented under CLIP/CLAPS and also with the LEP. If 80 per cent of the children are able to perform the competencies of literacy and numeracy the school is graded as 'A' and if the number of children whose performance is between 60-79 it is 'B' grade and 50-59 is C grade and below 49 is 'D' grade. The schools grades are being displayed in all the schools for public reference. This is what is expected under the LEP, to what extent the basic activities of LEP are being implemented and grading schools is done to enable the project to bring necessary changes in the performance and improve it better in the context of quality improvement of Primary Education.

Training Programme on Conducting School Complex Activities

This is an important training programme for the proper conduction of school complex activities. In this programme, the role of the complex chairman is high lighted. He is entrusted with monitoring of primary schools. School complex is an opportunity for teachers to expose their talents. Brain storming discussions to develop pedagogy will take place.

In-service Training Policies in the Future

1. In-service training should be considered as both a right and a duty of educators. Any in-service training policy should guarantee a minimum of training opportunities for all teachers.

2. In-service training should be organized to a greater extent within educational establishments and through team work, with the active participation of the teachers themselves in defining the programme.

3. Special attention should be paid to teachers at the beginning of their career, since the initial positions that they will hold and tasks they will perform will have a decisive effect on the remainder of their training and career.

4. Mechanisms which make it possible for pre-service training to benefit from the experience gained in in-service training should be set up in order to give future

teachers a opportunity to become acquainted with the problems encountered and the solutions adopted in a professional context.

5. In-service training should be developed through the medium of professional support services, which have been conceived as centers of assistance in solving problems, and to which all teachers should have access.

6. Special priority should be given to the in-service training and education of those involved in the management, supervision and evaluation of teachers in order to enable them not only to play an administrative or supervisory role, but also to provide pedagogical guidance.

7. Teacher trainers and teacher training institutes should play an essential part in the process of strengthening the role of teachers and actively participate in their in-service training.

8. Urgent action should be undertaken in areas where teachers are under qualified and un- trained. Besides, being a means of certification, this urgent action should strengthen the teachers' professional competence and upgrade their knowledge of current developments in pedagogy and subject matter, thus making in-service education a continuous process of educational renewal.

RESEARCH STUDIES

The following are some of the research findings related to in-service training programmes.

In-service Training Programmes and Attitude of Teachers

Mama, K. (1980) has found that teachers expressed positive opinion on training programmes. This study is confined to secondary teachers of Maharashtra.

Singh, S. (1980), found that the input of the training programme changed the attitude of the teachers making it more favorable than the previous one.

Gadgil, A.V. (1981) found that fifty seven percent of teachers did not see any advantage in Orientation programmes.

SCERT, Andhra Pradesh (1987), found that the participants felt that the training programme was good and helped in developing knowledge about new concepts. They felt motivated to implement most of the teaching strategies during the course.

Vyas, J.C. (1991), has found that the performance of the teachers trained under the PMOST was found to be better than those who were not trained under the PMOST in some areas.

Sharma, Subhash Chandra (1992) has found that 85 per cent of teachers could get their concepts (in their subjects) clear through in-service education. 76.5 per cent teachers could find a change in their attitudes due to the in-service education programmes.

K.S.N.Raju, (2008) has found that there is high attitude of teachers towards in-service training programmes.

S. Ratna Kumari (2008), has found that the teachers opined that children's performance has increased after the training programmes.

SCERT, Andhra Pradesh (2009) found that teachers perceived in-service training programmes as important and as which contributes to their professional growth.

Shyni Duggal of Jamia Milia has found that:

(i) Majority of teachers responded that their respective Head Masters nominated them on mandatory basis; and

(ii) The range of time spent on academic activities in one-week programmes was 42.73 per cent to 50.49 per cent.

In-service Training Programmes and Their Relevancy

Naga Raju, C.S. (1982) found that there was need for in-service training programmes. But majority of the trained teachers were not satisfied with the training they received.

S.Eswaran and Ajit Singh in their study sponsored by All India Primary Teachers Federation found that nearly 94 per cent of the teachers are of the opinion that the content given in the training programmes is relevant to certain extent only.

In-service Training Programmes and Performance of Children

Sarva Siksha Abhiyan, Andhra Pradesh (2005) found that due to training programmes given to teachers, children's performance increased.

Sarva Siksha Abhiyan, Andhra Pradesh (2006) found that children's listening and understanding ability has increased due to radio lessons.

Sarva Siksha Abhiyan, Andhra Pradesh (2006-07) found that children were able to attain CLIP competencies.

Sarva Siksha Abhiyan, Chandigarh (2006-07) found that CAL programme has increased the pupils' achievement.

In-service Training Programmes and Qualification

Venkateswara Rao and B.B. Rao (2004), in their study on In-service Training Programmes found that D.Ed. teachers, have shown better performance than B.Ed. and M.Ed. teachers that implies that teachers with B.Ed. have shown high attitude than teachers with M.Ed.

In-service Training Programmes and Expectations of Teachers

Gadgil, A.V. (1981) found that most of the teachers desired to have continuing education/orientation in school subjects to get mastery over them.

SCERT, AP, (2009) found that teachers felt the resource persons of these training programmes should be more rigorously trained and they should totally substitute lecture methods by activity method and adopt participatory approach. They also felt that these training programmes should include topics like games, physical exercises, organization of the school, problem solving and teaching English language.

In-service Training Programmes and Quality in Education

SCERT, Andhra Pradesh (2009) found that training programmes were effective in bringing out the needed momentum among teachers and community in improving enrollment and retention. At the same time, it was also found that they were ineffective in improving the quality of education.

In-service Training Programmes and Teacher Experience

Sharma, Subhash Chandra, in his study found that teachers in the age group of 45 to 50 years or with experience of more than 15 years were having less and unproductive impact of in-service education.

In-service Training Programmes and Gender

SCERT, Andhra Pradesh (2009) found that both men and women showed higher attitude towards in-service training programmes, women are rating slightly higher than their male counterparts.

DPEP has also conducted some studies on in-service training programmes. DPEP was started in 1994 in 42 districts in seven states. The main concern of the DPEP is to improve quality of primary education. The focus has been on establishing a pedagogical vision of child centered, activity based teaching-learning in class rooms. DPEP Resource group on teacher training was established in NCERT.

Studies conducted by Jangira and Yadav (1994) in DPEP districts reveal that learning achievement of pupils in Reading and Mathematics is abysmally low. The situation is a cause for deep concern and raises a number of issues: Are teachers qualified to teach? Are they appropriately trained to teach? Is teacher policy of different State governments conducive to promote and sustain teachers' motivation for good performance? Are there works and career rewards for promoting their performance? How do teachers perceive their social, economic and professional status? The study was conducted to find answers to these questions.

A training design for training of teachers and other functionaries was developed. Instead of one short training, the design envisages recurring trainings for teachers and their trainers. Excellent training material was developed.

Though several studies were conducted on the effectiveness of in-service training programmes, still there is vacuum in the field so that the present study has been taken. No previous study is comprehensive in its approach. No study was taken up taking the sample from teachers working in West Godavari district. Studies were not conducted taking the variables:

1. urban, rural and tribal; and
2. gender variable i.e., male and female.

In the present context where more focus was given on primary education, this study is supposed to be an important one and may show the direction for the effectiveness of in-service training programmes. It is to be concluded, after the study of theoretical perspectives of in-service training programmes and the review of research studies related to in-service training programmes to teachers, that a study is required to find out the attitude of teachers towards in-service training programmes.

3 Methodology of Research

The formidable problem that follows the task of defining the research problem is the preparation of the design of the research project, popularly known as the 'Research Design'. Research is a systematic enquiry seeking facts through objective and verifiable methods in order to discover the relationship among them and to deduce the broad principles or laws from them.

A research design is the arrangement of conditions for collection and analysis of data in a manner that aims to combine relevance to research purpose with economy in procedure (Clair Selltiz, et.al., 1962). In fact the research design is the conceptual structure within which research is conducted. Important features of a research design are: it is a plan that specifies the source and types of information relevant to the research problem; it is a strategy specifying which approach will be used for gathering and analyzing the data; and it also includes the time and cost budgets since most studies are done under these two constraints.

Research design is needed because it facilitates the smooth sailing of various research operations, thereby making research as efficient as possible yielding maximal information with minimal expenditure of effort, time and money. Research design stands for advanced planning of the methods to be adopted for collecting the relevant data and the techniques to be used in their analysis, keeping in view the objectives of the research and the availability of staff, time and money. Research design, in fact, has a great bearing on the reliability of the results arrived at and as such it constitutes the firm foundation of the entire edifice of the research work.

Planning is a necessary step for a good research as it is the heart of any research. Therefore the very success of a research work depends upon collecting the necessary information. Several methods of collecting information are developed to assist the researcher. Every survey expert has his own ideas of selecting the best method of collecting information. But the method may not be uniform to all. Selection of the method depends on the type of the information to be gathered and the source of information to be consulted. For the present study, normative survey method is chosen.

Survey means viewing and interpreting things vigorously and comprehensively. Now-a-days, survey method is a popular way of collecting data and analyzing the results statistically and systematically. This method is suitable to this study as this one is a status study.

The present investigation falls under broad category of descriptive research. Descriptive research is concerned with hypothesis formulation and testing the analysis of the relationships between the non manipulated variables and the development of generalizations. In descriptive research variables that exist or have already occurred are selected and observed. This process is described as causal-comparative research.

Further descriptive research reveals, what is describing, recording, analyzing and interpreting conditions that exist. It involves some type of comparison and attempts to discover relationships between existing variables. By virtue of the methods of research employed, the investigation is mainly survey type. The survey is an important type of study. It requires expert and imaginative planning, careful analysis and interpretations of the data gathered and logical and skillful reporting of the findings. (*John W. Best* and *James V. Khan*).

In this chapter, the following aspects have been discussed in detail, which are concerned with the design of the present study. Research procedures followed include the operational definitions of the different terms used, the various hypotheses that were framed for verification and the rationale of these hypotheses. Selection of the sample includes the sampling technique, and the selection of sample according to different variables. Selection of research tool covers selection of collection of data, description of tool selected, testing its suitability for the present study and the procedure followed in the administration of the tool to collect the data required for this study.

OPERATIONAL DEFINITION OF KEY TERMS

The operational definitions of the important key terms used in the present study on "A Study of the Effectiveness of In-service Training Programmes imparting at Primary School level" are discussed and defined herewith:

Study: Study refers to a systematic investigation which is objective and research oriented.

Effectiveness: Effectiveness refers to conducting a training programme in an effective manner to get the desired result.

In-service: Teachers working in schools are called as in-service teachers.

Training: Training means to "teach a specified skill by practice" or "a process of learning skill".

Primary Teachers: Teachers working in Primary Schools dealing with I to V Classes are called as primary teachers.

Primary school: School having classes from I to V is called as primary school.

Gender: Gender refers to male and female teachers.

Locality: Locality refers to rural, urban and tribal areas. Primary schools located in villages are termed as rural area schools. Schools located in towns and cities are called as urban area schools. Schools located in tribal areas as notified by the government, where scheduled tribes population is more are called as tribal schools.

Educational Qualifications: Educational qualifications refer to whether the teacher is having graduation (or Intermediate) qualification or a post graduation qualification.

Experience: Experience refers to whether the teacher is having 15 years or less service or more than 15 years of service.

VARIABLES OF THE STUDY

Variables are the conditions or characteristics that the experimenter manipulates, controls or observes. There are mainly three types of variables, namely, independent, dependent and intervening. The independent variables are those variables which do not change on manipulation by the experimenter. The dependent variables are those variables which change on manipulation done by the experimenter. The intervening variables are those variables which are dependent on both independent variables and dependent variables.

For the present study the following variables are chosen:

(i) Working Area Variables Urban, Rural and Tribal areas

(ii) Gender Variables Male teachers and Female teachers.

(iii) Qualification Variables
Teachers having Degree (or Intermediate) or Post graduation

(iv) Experience Variables
Teachers having 15 years or less service and Teachers having more than 15 years of service

The following is the rationale for selecting the above said variables:

1. Male Teachers *Vs.* Female Teachers

In government schools, the number of male teachers and female teachers is almost same. Female teachers are considered to be more patient and affectionate towards children than male teachers. They are considered to be more suitable for teaching primary classes. At the same time they may face some constraints in attending the training programmes because of the venue change. Also male and female teachers differ in their psychological aspects. Therefore, gender is taken as a variable to observe the difference in attitude between male and female teachers.

2. Rural *Vs.* Urban *Vs.* Tribal Area Teachers

Facilities available for teachers, working in urban areas, rural areas and tribal areas, are totally different. Teachers working in urban areas enjoy more facilities than those of rural and tribal areas. Schools in urban areas have good facilities such as drinking water, electricity, computers etc. which will help in effective transformation of teaching — learning process. Also, training centers in urban areas possess all the facilities and resources when compared to rural and tribal areas. Now a days, many teachers working in tribal areas are shuttling from towns which may affect their attitude to work in those areas. Pupils' attendance is also generally high in urban schools. Therefore working area variable is taken up to study whether there is any significant difference in attitude in teachers working in these areas.

3. Graduate (or Intermediate) Teachers *Vs.* Post-Graduate Teachers

In primary schools, teachers having different qualifications such as Intermediate plus D.Ed., graduation with D.Ed. or B.Ed. or with post graduation or even higher qualifications. Higher qualification may sometimes lead to frustration in job satisfaction. Sometimes, teachers with higher qualification may feel that training programmes are not necessary for them in terms of content transaction. In this context, qualification variable is taken up for consideration.

4. Teachers with Less Than 15 Years of Experience *Vs.* Teachers with More Than 15 Years of Experince

Experience is a very important criterion in effective teaching. Especially in primary schools, teachers having more experience may deal very patiently and effectively with children. They are well aware of the individual differences among the children. At the same time, more experience generally implies higher age. This may affect in their attitude in attending the training programmes. In this context this variable is taken up for consideration.

HYPOTHESES OF THE STUDY

Hypotheses are the most important aspects in a research process. It is a tentative supposition or provisional guess which seems to explain the situation under observation. A hypothesis is a tentative generalization the validity of which remains to be seen. In its most elementary stage the hypothesis may be any hunch, guess, imaginative idea which becomes the basis for further investigation. Hypothesis reflects the research worker's guess as to the probable outcome of the experiments. Formulating a hypothesis about the problem is a precondition. In the absence of hypothesis, the collection of data becomes aimless. A good hypothesis shall be in agreement with the observed facts, with laws of nature and is an expert statement. It should be stated in simplest possible terms and shall secure an answer to the problem.

There are different forms of hypothesis namely Null Form, Prediction form, Declarative form, Question form etc. The following hypotheses are formulated based on the variables and the objectives of the study. These were stated in 'Null Hypothesis' form. The Null Form is preferred by most of the experienced research personnel. This form of statement more rapidly defines the mathematical model to be utilized in the statistical test of the hypothesis. The Null Hypothesis states that there is no significant relationship between two or more parameters. It concerns to a judgment at whether apparent differences or relationships are true or whether they merely result from sampling error.

Keeping the objectives in view, the following Null hypotheses were formulated:

1. There is no high attitude of primary teachers towards the effectiveness of in-service training programmes.
2. There is no significant difference in the attitude of male and female primary teachers towards the effectiveness of in-service training programmes.
3. There is no significant difference in the attitude of urban and rural primary teachers towards the effectiveness of in-service training programmes.
4. There is no significant difference in the attitude of urban and tribal primary teachers towards the effectiveness of in-service training programmes.
5. There is no significant difference in the attitude of rural and tribal primary teachers towards the effectiveness of in-service training programmes.
6. There is no significant difference in the attitude of graduate (or intermediate) and post-graduate primary teachers towards the effectiveness of in-service training programmes.
7. There is no significant difference in the attitude of more experienced (above 15 years) and less experienced (less than or equal to 15 years) primary teachers towards the effectiveness of in-service training programmes.

SAMPLE OF THE STUDY

A sample is a smaller representation of the larger whole. A sample contains primarily sampling units and a slice of the population representing the universe. A sample must possess the following essential characteristics to provide accurate results. They are representativeness, adequacy, homogeneity, lack of bias, smallness in size, accuracy and completeness. After finalizing the variables, consideration was given to whether the entire population is to be made the subject for data collection or a particular group is to be selected as representative of the whole population.

As a sample is a slice of the population, the population for this study refers to all the in-service teachers working in government schools in West Godavari District.

Sampling is the easiest method of investigation. The purpose of sampling is to draw inferences concerning the universe. According to Goode and Hatt, "a sample as the name implies, is a smaller representation of a larger whole". Bogardus defined sampling as the selection of certain percentage of a group items according to a pre-determined plan. The sample should give a true picture of the population from which it is drawn. In any research, various methods are utilized for selection of sample.

The selection of a group as a representative of the whole population was found to be more convenient and suitable. The technique leads to a considerable saving of time, effort and finance. The number of students selected will be small in order to make a detailed and intensive study. This generally leads to more accurate and reliable results. As this sampling has many advantages, it was selected for the collection of data.

In any social research, various methods are utilized for selection and drawing of samples. After a detailed study of all these methods and considering the variables selected for the research work, the stratified sampling was found to be most suitable.

In stratified sampling technique, the entire population is divided into two smaller homogeneous groups and then the sample is selected within each group. Every sampling unit in the population is placed in one of the strata prior to the selection of the sample so that the sum of the strata is identical with the population. Stratified sampling method has certain merits and advantages as a technique of sampling. Auckof has rightly said that stratified sampling enables the researcher to make a comparison of properties of the strata as well as to estimate population characteristics.

In stratified sampling technique, the investigator has greater control over the selection of the sample when compared with random sampling. In random sampling technique although every group has a chance of being selected and included in the sample, there is every possibility and sometimes it does happen that certain important groups are left unrepresented. But, in stratified sampling technique, no important group is likely to be left out.

Stratified sampling is the ideal one when comparison between different variables has to be made. For example, if comparison has to be made between teachers working in rural, urban and tribal areas, it would be very difficult to select the required number of units through any other technique of sampling. If any other technique is used, the problem of bias and prejudice creeps in.

Replacement of units is also possible in the stratified sampling technique. Normally, if a particular unit is not accessible for a study, it is difficult to replace it by any other technique but in this technique it is possible. Stephen states that stratification automatically brings about a replacement of persons lost to the sample by persons of the same stratum, thus partly correcting the bias that would result if there were no replacement of units. As the entire population is divided into particular strata it is easy and convenient to replace an inaccessible case by an accessible one.

In stratified sampling technique, much depends on the stratification process. The following precautions were taken while stratifying the population; the variables involved in the study were taken note of, care was taken to see that each stratum in the universe was large enough in size so that the selection of items could be done on random basis, the strata formed were definite and clear cut, each stratum was free from influence of the other so that there would be no overlapping.

Before actually selecting the sample, certain fundamental principles were considered to make the sample scientific and clear cut.

Firstly, the 'universe' was clearly defined. In the technical phraseology of research, the whole population out of which the samples are selected is known as the 'universe'. For the present research work, the universe includes all the teachers working in government primary schools in West Godavari district. The study was limited to a particular geographical area to facilitate appropriate sample selection and to avoid bias and prejudice.

Secondly, decision has to be made about the units of the sample. A unit of sample may be a house, a family, a group of individuals or a single individual. A good unit should possess the following characteristics:

(i) ***Clarity:*** The unit should be clearly defined in unambiguous terms. This would make the study easy and efficient. For the present research work, a sampling unit was defined as a teacher working in a primary school in West Godavari district.

(ii) ***Suitability:*** A good unit should be well suited to the problem under study. Since the problem is to find out the effectiveness of in-service training programmes imparting at primary level, the unit selected is well suited to the problem.

(iii) ***Accessibility:*** The unit selected should be easily accessible to the researcher. If the units selected are difficult to reach and if the researcher fails to

make use of them the study would be vitiated. The selected sample unit, i.e., teacher working in primary school is easily accessible since he/she could be approached in any primary school.

Thirdly, consideration should be given to the preparation of the source list. This is an important factor that makes representative selection possible. A source list is the list which contains the names of the units of the universe from which the sample may be selected. It may exist even before the beginning of the project or it may be prepared afresh by the investigator himself. Without a source list, study through a sampling technique is not possible. For the present research work a source list consisting of the names of schools in west Godavari district was used. Care was taken to see that the source list was up-to-date and valid and there was no repetition of the names of the schools. This source list was found to be relevant and suitable because it included primary schools as the study deals with the teachers working in primary schools.

Besides considering these principles, it is extremely important to think about the size of the sample to be selected. If the sample is either too small or too large, it will make the study difficult and also make the results untenable. According to Patten, 'an optimum sample in survey is one which fulfils the requirements of effective representativeness, reliability and flexibility'. The sample should be small enough to avoid intolerable sampling error.

The size of the sample for the present research work was decided after considering the following factors:

Since an intensive study was planned, a very large number of samples were not selected. In case of an intensive study, very large numbers of samples were not useful as they involve huge consumption of resources. A smaller sample was most convenient.

The size and selection of samples will also be influenced by the nature of the universe. If the universe is homogeneous even a small- sized sample may yield dependable and required results. If the universe is heterogeneous, small sized sample may not be used. In case of the present study, the heterogeneous universe was split into smaller homogeneous strata and the samples were selected from these strata.

The investigator needs to determine the number of groups to be formed. In case the number of groups proposed is large, the size of the samples shall have to large so that every group should be of proper size and suit the requirement of the study. In case the number of groups proposed is small, even small-sized samples can fulfill the requirements. In case of the present study, the groups into which the universe was divided are male teachers and female teachers, teachers working in urban, rural and tribal areas, teachers having B.A. (or Intermediate) and M.A. qualifications, teachers having 15 years or less service and more than 15 years of service. Since the number of groups was moderate, a reasonable sample was selected from each of these groups.

The size of the sample is also governed by the size of the tools to be used. In case the tools are short and the questions asked pertain to certain limited factors, a large sample can be selected. In case the tools are large and the questions are complicated the sample should be small in size so that, from administrative point of view, the investigator may not be put to unnecessary troubles. In the present study, the tool was a questionnaire with 25 statements, a moderate sample was selected.

The sampling technique also determines the size of the sample. When random sampling technique is used, the sample has to be large. On the other hand, if samples are selected through stratified sampling technique, the reliability can be achieved even with the small-sized samples.

After taking into consideration all these factors, which influence the size of the sample, it was decided that an ideal sample would consist of one hundred and fifty teachers. This is small enough to avoid intolerable sampling errors and large enough to draw perfect conclusions.

After deciding about the sampling method and size of the sample, the universe was divided into different strata. The variables chosen for the study were considered in dividing the universe. The variables chosen were male versus female teachers, urban versus rural versus tribal areas' teachers, teachers with B.A. (or Intermediate) versus M.A. qualification and teachers with 15 years or less experience versus more than 15 years of experience.

Following the sampling procedure, 150 primary teachers were selected as sample for the present study. The total sample of 150 primary school teachers consists of the following number of variables:

Male teachers-85, female teachers-65; teachers working in urban schools-50, rural schools-50, tribal schools-50; teachers with graduation or Intermediate-112, post graduates-38; teachers with 15 years or less experienced-102, more than 15 years of experience-48.

In the present study, the stratum divided is represented in the following table.

<table>
<tr><td colspan="6">Total
(150)</td></tr>
<tr><td colspan="3">Male
(85)</td><td colspan="3">Female
(65)</td></tr>
<tr><td colspan="2">Urban
(50)</td><td colspan="2">Rural
(50)</td><td colspan="2">Tribal
(50)</td></tr>
<tr><td colspan="3">Graduates
(112)</td><td colspan="3">Post Graduates
(38)</td></tr>
<tr><td colspan="3">More experienced
(48)</td><td colspan="3">Less experienced
(102)</td></tr>
</table>

The study is confined to West Godavari district only. For the study purpose 6 mandals were selected of which 2 were urban mandals, 2 were rural mandals and 2 were tribal mandals. The selection of mandals was based on Random sampling method. In each mandal, 25 teachers were selected covering 10 to 12 schools. The selection of schools was random.

The following are the details of total sample involved in the study.

(i)	No. of mandals	:	6
(ii)	Urban mandals	:	2
(iii)	Rural mandals	:	2
(iv)	Tribal mandals	:	2
(iv)	Teachers from each mandal	:	25
(v)	Total no. of teachers	:	$6 \times 25 = 150$

The list of mandals and the schools from where the data was collected was appended.

TOOLS OF THE STUDY

Research tools are the sole factors in determining the sound data and in having accurate conclusions about the problem on hand. The conclusions ultimately help in providing remedial measures to the problem concerned.

The selection and use of tools can be done in two ways. The first one is to construct a tool independently by the researcher for his own study. The second way of selection and use of tool is right selection of tools from already standardized ones available in the field of study. Here also it involves a tedious job in locating the tools and identifying their usefulness to the study on hand. Even then this technique is very useful when a research work involves a good number of variables and resources are scarce. Some people believe that some of the instruments available don't measure to their standards. Hence, new ones. In some instances consideration should be given to the logic of the situation. Lacking the time and financial resources, many researchers can not expect to produce a better instrument. In these cases, the most logical procedure that one can follow is to choose the best instrument available for the purpose.

Considering the flaws and merits of the selection of tools in either way, the researcher is interested in using self prepared tool for this purpose. After preparing this scale, it was administered on a small sample of teachers. When analysis of data was made, the reliability was established. Hence this scale was selected for final administration.

In this, the researcher wants to study the effectiveness of in-service training programmes imparting at primary level. Success of any training programme depends on the attitude of teachers. Attitude denotes the inner feeling or belief of a person towards a particular phenomenon.

The method of inferring attitude is Questionnaire or Opinionnaire. Questionnaire refers to a device for seeking answers to questions by using a form which the respondent fills himself. According to Barr, Davis and Johnson, questionnaire is a systematic compilation of questions or statements that are submitted to a sampling of population from which information is designed. It is yet the most flexible of tools in collecting both quantitative and qualitative information. Careful preparation of a questionnaire takes a great deal of time and hard work.

A questionnaire consists of a number of questions or statements printed or typed in a definite order on a form or set of forms. The tool is easy to administer, free from the bias of the interviewer and respondents have adequate time to give well thought out answers. Before actual administration of the questionnaire, a pilot study was conducted for testing the reliability and validity of the statements in the questionnaire. Here pilot study was proved to be very useful.

Initially the researcher prepared 35 statements reflecting the attitude of primary teachers towards the effectiveness of in-service training programmes. The statements are based on the impact of different in-service training programmes on effective class room teaching methodology and there by the output observed from the pupils. These statements are carefully prepared and then these are presented to some subject experts in the field of education such as senior teachers, Mandal Educational Officers and DIET lecturers for their comments. They evaluated the items chosen for inclusion in the instrument in terms of whether they are relevant to the topic area and unambiguous in implication. They suggested for deletion of 6 questions. After this, Item Analysis approach is also followed for developing the tool. This is treated under three heads:

1. item selection;
2. item difficulty; and
3. item validity.

Here the tool prepared was given to a group of respondents. After administering the test, the total scores are calculated for everyone. Items are then analyzed. Their validity is established. By this process, another four statements are deleted from the tool. By this process, standardization of the tool is done. Finally, "Effectiveness of In-service Training Programmes Scale" is finalized with 25 statements.

The scale was a structured one. Here responses of the informants are limited to the stated alternatives. Here the scale used is a closed type or restricted type. It provides for making 'yes', 'undecided' or 'no', a short response from a list of suggested responses. It is easy to respond, takes little time, keeps the respondent on the track of the subject and obtained responses can easily be tabulated and analyzed. In order to make the scale effective and to ensure quality to the replies received, the sequence of statements is given importance in preparing the scale. A proper sequence of statements is followed. The statement-sequence was clear and smoothly-moving, meaning thereby that the relation of one statement to another should be readily apparent to the respondent, with statements that are easiest to answer being put in the beginning. The first few questions are particularly important because they are likely to influence the attitude of the respondent and in seeking his desired cooperation. Statements of a personal character, statements that put too great a strain on the memory or intellect of the respondent or statements related to personal characteristics are carefully avoided in preparing the scale. Statements framed were impartial in order not to give a biased picture of the true state of affairs. The statements framed are in a simple manner so that the respondent can easily understand the statement. After the pilot survey, the validity and reliability of the scale are established.

Keeping all the issues in view, "Effectiveness of In-service Training Programmes Scale" was finally developed with 25 statements to collect the data from teachers on the effectiveness of training programmes conducted. The scale for teachers consisted of the teachers' personal information like name, gender, educational qualifications, school working, whether the teacher is working in rural, urban or tribal area and experience of the teacher. Besides the information, the scale consisted of 25 close-ended statements with three point scale yes/undecided/no.

The scale broadly consisted of statements on the following aspects:

1. Teacher motivation and interest in attending the training programmes.
2. The effectiveness of the training programmes in realizing the objectives in the classroom.
3. The way of conducting of training programmes such as arrangement of physical facilities at the training centre etc.

The rationale behind choosing statements on the above aspects is that they will be helpful in determining the attitude of the teacher towards in-service training programmes. In training programmes, orientation is given on some new methodology and the teachers implemented those methodologies in the class rooms. Basing on the methodology of the class room transaction, there might be change in the behaviour of the children, regularity in coming to school, new inputs received by them, the attitude of parents on the performance of their children, all these things will determine the attitude of teachers towards in-service training programmes. Sometimes training programmes conducted in school days may be detrimental to the normal functioning of schools which will affect the academic performance of the children. This may also affect the attitude of teachers towards training programmes.

Procedure for Scoring

The Scale contained 25 statements of which 23 are of positive and 2 are of negative polarity.

The scoring procedure for items of positive polarity is as follows:

Response	Score
Yes	3
Undecided	2
No	1

The scoring procedure for items of negative polarity is as follows:

Response	Score
Yes	1
Undecided	2
No	3

The maximum and the minimum score of the scale is 75 and 25 respectively.

ADMINISTRATION OF THE TOOL

The investigator personally visited all the schools. The teachers were clearly told the purpose of administering the "Effectiveness of In-service Training Programmes Scale". They were even informed that this tool is intended for a limited purpose, that is for the purpose of submitting dissertation in partial fulfillment of the requirement for the award of M.Phil. Degree. The teachers were given the "Effectiveness of In-service Training Programmes Scale" and were requested to answer it. They were given sufficient time. They were asked to respond to all the items by putting a tick (_/) mark against their choice from the given alternatives. They were informed that there is no right or wrong answer and the scale is intended to know the attitude of teachers towards in-service training programmes. After completion, the Scales were collected from the respondents.

Analysis of Data

Analysis of the data is the most important part of all stages of research. The right interpretation of the data depends on the expertise and skill of the researcher. It should be done by the investigator and should not be entrusted to anyone. This is the heart of the research report. Analysis and interpretation of the data has to be done with the help of the text, tables and figures. Analysis of data means studying the tabulated material in order to determine inherent facts or meanings. It involves breaking down complex factors into simple ones and putting the parts in new arrangements for the purpose of interpretation.

The first step in the analysis of data is a critical examination of the data. This includes the researcher to think and analyze the data in the next method of analysis of data i.e. coding. Coding is an important process in the process of research. Coding involves assigning symbols to each response, the purpose of which is to translate raw data into symbols. This depends on proper coding of responses. As far as possible, the researcher should code the data. This will help in improving the quality of data collection.

Tabulation is a means of recording classification in a compact form in such a way so as to facilitate comparisons. Data is arranged in rows and columns to facilitate mathematical and statistical operations. It is of great help in the analysis and interpretation of data. While tabulating the data, the purpose of the study has to be kept in mind.

The method of analysis chosen for a particular study depends upon the nature of objectives, hypotheses to be tested, the purpose and use of the study. Statistical methods are mathematical techniques used to facilitate the interpretation of numerical data secured from groups of individual or group of observation or a single individual. A basic knowledge of mathematical techniques becomes inevitable for research workers, for systematic analysis and accurate and precise interpretation of data.

For the present study titled "A Study of the Effectiveness of In-service Training Programmes Imparting at Primary School Level" several statistical techniques were used to perform the analysis. After collecting the data from working teachers through self made Scale, the analysis was performed keeping in view of the objectives framed, hypotheses formulated, type of data collected, type of tool used etc., The highest attitude score is 75 and the lowest attitude score is 25. For this purpose, mean, standard deviation, critical ratio, normal probability characteristics etc., were employed. Degree of attitude is calculated using the normal probability method.

Score	Degree of Attitude
Up to 31	Low
32 to 56	Average
56 to 75	High

Hypothesis 1

"There is no high attitude of primary teachers towards the effectiveness of in-service training programmes"

To test the validity of hypothesis 1, the total scores of the sample were used to calculate the mean. The results are as follows:

Table 4.1: Level of Attitude of Primary Teachers towards the Effectiveness of In-service Training Programmes at Primary Level

Sample	Sample Size	Mean
Whole	150	68.25

As per the mean value of the whole sample, the teachers are possessing high degree of positive attitude towards in-service training programmes at primary level.

So, the hypothesis that "there is no high attitude of primary teachers towards the effectiveness of in-service training programmes" can be rejected.

Hypothesis 2

"There is no significant difference in the attitude of male and female primary teachers towards the effectiveness of in-service training programmes."

The following calculations were made to test the validity of hypothesis 2. The results are as follows:

Table 4.2: Comparison of Attitude Male and Female Primary Teachers towards the Effectiveness of In-Service Training Programmes

Variable	Sample Size	Mean	S.D.	Mean Difference	Critical Ratio
Male	85	67.86	4.87	0.91	1.28 *
Female	65	68.77	3.86		

Critical value at 0.05 level is 1.96.

* Not significant at 0.05 level.

From the Table 4.2, it is evident that there is no significant difference in the attitude of male and female primary teachers towards the effectiveness of in-service training programmes. Both have high level of attitude towards in-service training programmes.

Therefore, the hypothesis "there is no significant difference in the attitude of male and female primary teachers towards the effectiveness of in-service training programmes" can be accepted.

Hypothesis 3

"There is no significant difference in the attitude of urban and rural primary teachers towards the effectiveness of in-service training programmes".

The following calculations were made to test the validity of hypothesis 3. The results are as follows:

Table 4.3: Comparison of Attitude of Urban and Rural Primary Teachers towards the Effectiveness of In-Service Training Programmes

Variable	Sample Size	Mean	S.D.	Mean Difference	Critical Ratio
Rural	50	68.82	4.34	1.20	1.46*
Urban	50	70.02	3.88		

Critical value at 0.05 level is 1.96.

* Not significant at 0.05 level.

From the Table 4.3, it is evident that there is no significant difference in attitude between teachers working in urban and rural areas. Both have high level of attitudes towards in-service training programmes.

Therefore, the hypothesis "there is no significant difference in the attitude of urban and rural primary teachers towards the effectiveness of in-service training programmes" can be accepted.

Hypothesis 4

"There is no significant difference in the attitude of urban and tribal primary teachers towards the effectiveness of in-service training programmes"

The following calculations are made to test the validity of hypothesis 4. The results are as follows:

Table 4.4: Comparison of Attitude of Urban and Tribal Primary Teachers towards the Effectiveness of In-Service Training Programmes

Variable	Sample Size	Mean	S.D.	Mean Difference	Critical Ratio
Urban	50	70.02	3.88	3.82	4.83@
Tribal	50	66.20	4.06		

Critical ratio at 0.01 level is 2.58.

@ Significant at 0.01 level.

From the Table 4.4, it is evident that there is significant difference in the attitude of the primary teachers working in urban and tribal areas towards in-service training programmes.

Therefore, the hypothesis "there is no significant difference in the attitude of urban and tribal primary teachers towards the effectiveness of in-service training programmes." can be rejected.

Hypothesis 5

"There is no significant difference in the attitude of rural and tribal primary teachers towards the effectiveness of in-service training programmes"

The following calculations are made to test the validity of hypothesis 5. The results are as follows:

From the Table 4.5, it is evident that there is significant difference in the attitude of rural and tribal teachers towards the effectiveness of in-service training programmes. At the same time both groups possess high level of attitude towards in-service training programmes.

Table 4.5: Comparison of Attitude of Rural and Tribal Primary Teachers towards the Effectiveness of In-Service Training Programmes

Variable	Sample Size	Mean	S.D.	Mean Difference	Critical Ratio
Rural	50	68.82	4.34	2.62	3.12@
Tribal	50	66.20	4.06		

Critical ratio at 0.01 level is 2.58.

@ Significant at 0.01 level.

Therefore, the hypothesis "there is no significant difference in the attitude of rural and tribal primary teachers towards the effectiveness of in-service training programmes." can be rejected.

Hypothesis 6

"There is no significant difference in the attitude of graduate (or intermediate) and post graduate primary teachers towards the effectiveness of in-service training programmes".

The following calculations are made to test the validity of hypothesis 6. The results are as follows:

Table 4.6: Comparison of the Attitude of Graduate and Post Graduate Primary Teachers Towards the Effectiveness of In-service Training

Variable	Sample Size	Mean	S.D.	Mean Difference	Critical Ratio
Graduates	112	68.39	4.33	0.55	0.61*
Post graduates	38	67.84	4.92		

Critical ratio at 0.05 level is 1.96.

* Not significant at 0.05 level.

From the Table 4.6, it is evident that there is no significant difference in attitude between graduate and post graduate primary teachers towards in-service training programmes. But both the groups have high level of attitude in-service training programmes.

Therefore, the hypothesis "there is no significant difference in the attitude of graduate and post graduate primary teachers towards the effectiveness of in-service training programmes." can be accepted.

Hypothesis 7

"There is no significant difference in the attitude of more experienced and less experienced primary teachers towards the effectiveness of in-service training programmes"

The following calculations are made to test the validity of hypothesis 7. The results are as follows:

Table 4.7: Comparison of the Attitude of More Experienced and Less Experienced Primary Teachers towards the Effectiveness of In-service Training Programmes

Variable	Sample Size	Mean	S.D.	Mean Difference	Critical Ratio
More Experienced	48	67.92	5.45	0.49	0.56*
Less Experienced	102	68.41	3.88		

Critical ratio at 0.05 level is 1.96.

* Not significant at 0.05 level.

From the Table 4.7 it is evident that both the groups of primary teachers are having high level of attitudes towards the effectiveness of in-service training programmes. Mean values shows that less experienced teachers have high level of attitude towards the effectiveness of in-service training programmes than that of more experienced teachers. But it is clearly evident that there is no significant difference between these two groups of teachers in the attitude towards the effectiveness of in-service training programmes.

Therefore, the hypothesis "there is no significant difference in the attitude of more experienced and less experienced primary teachers towards the effectiveness of in-service training programmes" can be accepted.

Summary, Findings Discussion and Conclusions

Summary

Primary education occupies a significant place in the reconstruction of a developing country like India. The National Policy on Education envisages free and compulsory education of satisfactory quality should be provided to all children up to the age of 14 years irrespective of caste, creed, sex, religion etc., before we enter the 21st century. The 83rd constitution amendment bill has been introduced to make the right to elementary education, a fundamental right of the child and the fundamental duty of the Government the recent right to education act which came into force further strengthened the right of the child to get free education with quality inputs. Hence there is need to equip the teachers with latest teaching inputs to provide quality education to the children of elementary stage.

The education commission of 1964-'66 also greatly emphasized on in-service education of primary teachers. The recent right to education act, 2009 also stressed on the need to provide 20 days of training programmes to the in-service teachers. These in-service training programmes may be on different aspects such as content oriented, methodology oriented on co-curricular and extra-curricular activities to be conducted in schools, on computer education etc., it is futile exercise if in-service training programmes are conducted in haphazard manner without identifying the needs of the teachers.

It is hoped that in-service training programmes help the teachers in getting: Refreshment in both content and methodology, Acquiring latest skills in teaching methodologies, Creativity in teaching, Well organization of class room activities, and Developing positive attitude towards teaching.

Further, the findings on effectiveness of in-service training programmes are supported not only by the theories of learning but also by empirical researches. On the theoretical front, we know that effective teaching takes place when the teacher is equipped with the latest strategies. In-service training programme is like a refreshing programme which generates active discussion among the teachers in the group. The individual teachers share their ideas with the group and come to an agreement on the latest methods. Also in-service training programmes will motivate the teachers. At the same time effectiveness of training programmes are based on several aspects such as need of the programme felt by the teachers, physical facilities provided at the training place, age and experience of the teachers, their qualifications and on several other factors.

If in-service training programmes are conducted in an effective manner, the out put in terms of teacher attitude will be good. Learning takes place from birth to death. So, even the most experienced teacher needs to update his knowledge by getting some in-service training. With these aspects under consideration, the present study of effectiveness of in-service training programmes imparting at primary school level has been taken up.

The following objectives are framed for the present study:

1. To find out the attitude of primary teachers towards the effectiveness of in-service training programmes.

2. To find out the difference in the attitude of male and female primary teachers towards the effectiveness of in-service training programmes.
3. To find out the difference in the attitude of urban and rural primary teachers towards the effectiveness of in-service training programmes.
4. To find out the difference in the attitude of urban and tribal primary teachers towards the effectiveness of in-service training programmes.
5. To find out the difference in the attitude of rural and tribal primary teachers towards the effectiveness of in-service training programmes.
6. To find out the difference in the attitude of graduate (or Intermediate) and post-graduate primary teachers towards the effectiveness of in-service training programmes.
7. To find out the difference in the attitude of more experienced (15 or more years of teaching experience) and less experienced primary teachers (less than 15 years of teaching experience) towards the effectiveness of in-service training programmes.

The Normative Survey Method was used in the present study to investigate the effectiveness of in-service training programmes imparting at primary school level.

Variables are necessary requisites for any worthwhile research for the purpose of comparison. For the present study, the researcher has considered these variables viz., *Location* — teachers working in rural, urban and tribal areas; *Gender* — male and female teachers; *Qualifications* — graduate or below and post graduate teachers; *Experience* — less experienced teachers(15 years of service or below) and more experienced teachers (above 15 years of service)

Hypotheses are guesses or tentative generalizations which provide basis to the whole study to be tested by facts.

For the present study, the hypothesis framed were:

1. There is no high attitude of primary teachers towards the effectiveness of in-service training programmes.
2. There is no significant difference in the attitude of male and female primary teachers towards the effectiveness of in-service training programmes.
3. There is no significant difference in the attitude of urban and rural primary teachers towards the effectiveness of in-service training programmes.
4. There is no significant difference in the attitude of urban and tribal primary teachers towards the effectiveness of in-service training programmes.
5. There is no significant difference in the attitude of rural and tribal primary teachers towards the effectiveness of in-service training programmes.
6. There is no significant difference in the attitude of graduate (or Intermediate) and post graduate primary teachers towards the effectiveness of in-service training programme.
7. There is no significant difference in the attitude of more experienced (having 15 years or more experience) and less experienced (having less than 15 years of experience) primary teachers towards the effectiveness of in-service training programmes.

A sample is a small group which represents all the traits and characteristics of the population. The teachers working in urban, rural and tribal areas in West Godavari District were selected as population. The stratified random sampling technique was used in selecting the sample. The sample size was 150 in-service teachers. Two mandals from each area are chosen. From each mandal, 25 teachers are selected from 10 to 12 schools. Mandals and schools have been selected by stratified random sampling technique.

A research tool is a tool used for the purpose of data collection. The tool used in the present study is a self-prepared questionnaire with 25 questions. Each question has three responses, 'yes', 'undecided' and 'no'. The purpose of the tool is to find out the attitude of primary teachers towards in-service training programmes imparting at primary school level.

For the analysis of data, suitable statistical techniques like mean, standard deviation and critical ratio were used. Normal Probability Theory is applied for arriving at significant levels.

CONCLUSIONS AND DISCUSSION

The present study was resulted in drawing the following conclusions which may be helpful in improving the attitude of teachers towards in-service training programmes at primary level and there by assessing their effectiveness.

1. ***There is a high attitude of primary teachers towards the effectiveness of in-service training programmes at primary level***

This result was supported by Mama K (1980), SCERT, Andhra Pradesh (1987), Vyas JC (1991), Sharma, Subhash Chandra (1992), Sarva Siksha Abhiyan, Andhra Pradesh (2005), K.S.N.Raju (2008) and S.Ratna Kumari (2008) and SCERT, Andhra Pradesh (2009). Shiny Duggal of Jamia Milia and Manoj Kumar Dash (2008) have not supported the result.

It is a good sign to see a high attitude of teachers towards in-service training programmes. In-service training programmes are considered very important to the teachers for updating their knowledge. There is no difference of opinion among educationists on this issue. Unless teachers too feel the same, the purpose of in-service training programmes will not be achieved. As the teachers are having high attitude towards in-service training programmes it implies that they show interest in attending the programmes and share their experiences with others. Whatever they learn from these training programmes, they sincerely implement them in their classroom teaching. Also the purpose of the in-service training programmes will be achieved because of their high positive attitude. With this right attitude, if utilized properly, the teachers will become good professionals and practitioners of latest methodology in their teaching. On analyzing the individual questions, many of the teachers express their displeasure on the conduct of training programmes. This may be due to lack of necessary physical facilities at the training centers. It is opined that water and electricity facilities are not properly taken care of. Also it is to be seen whether chairs and tables are sufficiently arranged for the teachers. At some places frequent power cut is felt by the teachers. This may be a reason for their displeasure towards training programmes. Further it is to be seen whether teachers are informed well in advance about the training programmes they have to attend. Also it is to be ascertained from the teachers themselves about the nature and type of training programmes they need. Also it is evident from the analysis that pupil's attendance is decreasing due to frequent training programmes to teachers. This is a point of serious concern. The very basic reason for conducting training programmes to teachers is to get a desirable change in teachers as well as pupils. Therefore pupils' attendance should increase with these training programmes. But this is not the case in all schools. So the reasons are to be found out. Also it is to be seen whether the resource persons are competent to deliver the goods. If the resource group is not so competent, the effect will fall on the whole programme and there by the attitude of teachers will be adversely affected towards training programmes. It is to be seen whether the training received by teachers is reflecting their classroom transaction. If the above discussed items are taken care of, the success of training programmes will be even better.

Evaluation of the outcome of in-service teacher training programme need to be integrated with evaluation of classroom teaching-learning process. So effective design of the evaluation of in-service training programme is quite essential for improving quality of teaching by teachers and learning by children. Teachers working at primary level must undergo recurring training on various aspects. Performance of teachers is reflected from the performance of children. So, all the programmes of in-service teachers should be evaluated for improving professional competency of teachers.

It is essential to identify the strength and weakness of the training programme; so that it can be improved from time to time i.e. evaluation should be constructive. Evaluation of the objectives of training programme is crucial. So techniques like written, oral, practical and observations should constitute integral part of it. During in-service training programmes, teachers need to be trained on various aspects like cooperative/collaborative matters, individualized instruction; alternative instructional materials etc. resource persons from state level may be invited on different themes, so that teachers will get an opportunity to interact with high level experts. It provides reinforcement to them in attending the session actively and contributing substantially. Each teacher attending the training session need to be observed and informed individually about their performance. Group work and group discussion followed by presentation should be made an integral part of training programme. It provides exposure to individual participants.

2. ***Male and Female primary teachers are possessing high attitude towards the effectiveness of in-service training programmes without any significant difference***

The above result was supported by SCERT, Andhra Pradesh (2009). Females have shown slightly higher rating than their male counterparts.

Both male teachers and female teachers are possessing high attitude towards in-service training programmes. At the same time female teachers have slightly showed higher attitude than male teachers. The reasons may be due to their relatively well settlement and security in life, their interest and patience which suit for the teaching profession. But the difference in attitude among male teachers and female teachers is not significant. Especially female teachers expressed their displeasure over the physical arrangement provided at the training centers. Some expressed their feeling that even toilet facilities are not properly arranged. A group of 50 teachers have to sit in a small room without proper seating arrangement. The department should take a note of these items for better conduction of training programmes. It was even noticed that the timings for the training programmes should be suitably arranged after due consultation with the teachers. Though female teachers showed high attitude towards training programmes, it is observed that some of them expressed disinterest in attending the programmes. This may be due to the disturbed daily routine. Also in majority of the schools, multi class and multi grade teaching is going on. That is, one teacher is handling more than one class. In this context if one teacher is away for attending the training programme, the burden of his/her classes falls on the other teacher. This also may be a reason for their reluctance to attend the training programmes. So it is the responsibility of the authorities to make some arrangement so that the school is not disturbed during trainings. Also for women teachers, special room for relaxation during lunch break or tea break may be provided. At some places, female teachers take their young kid with them to their school. In training programmes it is not possible to do so as there will be no room for keeping their kids. If such an arrangement is made possible, the attitude of these female teachers towards training programmes will be even high. The department should think in this direction also.

3. *Primary teachers working in urban and rural areas are possessing high attitude towards the effectiveness of in-service training programmes without any significant difference*

Generally, in urban areas, availability of physical facilities such as transportation, power facility will be more when compared to rural areas. Also visits and monitoring of the higher officials will be more than that of other areas. Availability of resources will be more in urban training centres. In rural and tribal areas, there is frequent power failure, lack of adequate facilities at training centers. In summer, it is very difficult to conduct training programmes without power. This also may result in the attitude of teachers. Now-a-days the process of urbanization is seen in all aspects. Many teachers are shuttling from towns to their work places. So, for teachers working in urban areas, there is no difficulty in attending the training programmes as the training center is situated in urban area itself. In urban areas, it is observed that, facilities are available at training centers. In quality aspect also, there is scope for availability of good resource people. Basing on the training programme, local college lecturers and professors may be invited for delivering guest lectures. State level resource persons will be available at these centers. There is less chance for power failure. So audio-visual equipment and multimedia facilities can be utilized in urban areas. The department should see that the same facilities should be provided at training centers in rural areas also. In urban training centres possibility of visits by district level officials will be more when compared to rural training centers. Visits by district level officials will boost up the morale of teachers. Therefore more visits by officials to rural centers is suggested. This will raise the attitude of the teachers towards in-service training programmes.

4. *Primary teachers working in urban and tribal areas are possessing high attitude towards the effectiveness of in-service training programmes with significant difference*

It is a good sign to see a high attitude of teachers working in urban and tribal areas towards in-service training programmes. Teachers working in urban areas have shown higher attitude than those of tribal areas and also the difference is significant. Better infrastructural facilities, congenial teaching-learning atmosphere, good teacher-student interaction, easy accessibility to library etc., availability of latest technology, good parent-teacher relation, regularity of children, regular monitoring by officers etc., may be the reason for higher attitude of teachers working urban area towards in-service training programmes. The situation in tribal areas may be quite contrary to that. Teacher has to suffer a lot to reach his school, more drop out rate of children, irregularity in attendance, lack of motivation in children, lack of proper co-operation from parents, some times irregularity of teachers may be the reasons for relatively low attitude towards training programmes. School monitoring is to be strengthened so that necessary guidance will be given to the teachers. To develop the attitude of teachers in tribal areas, focus is to be given on the quality of training programmes. Good resource persons to be trained up, guest lectures to be arranged, frequent visits to be made by district officials and at the same time it is to be seen to what extent the input given in training programmes is being implemented in classroom transaction. Also focus is to be given on special methods to be adopted in tribal area schools.

5. *Primary teachers working in rural and tribal areas are possessing high attitude towards the effectiveness of in-service training programmes with significant difference*

It is observed that teachers working in rural and tribal areas have shown high attitude towards in-service training programmes. But teachers working in rural schools have shown higher attitude than those working in tribal areas and difference is significant.

In order to develop the attitude of teachers in tribal areas focus is to be given on the classroom transaction, strengthening of Academic Monitoring Committees; innovative activities to motivate the children, joyful learning etc., at training centers in tribal areas, physical facilities are to be provided. Provision of working lunch especially in rural and tribal areas will play a vital role in developing the attitude of teachers towards in-service training programmes. The teachers come from far away places to attend the training programmes. In rural and tribal areas good meals, hotels may not be available. Hence working lunch serves the purpose.

6. ***Both graduate (or Intermediate) and post graduate primary teachers are having high attitude towards the effectiveness of in-service training programmes without any significant difference***

Graduate (or Intermediate) teachers have shown slightly higher attitude than those of teachers with Post Graduation qualification. The reason may be due to the inner feeling or dissatisfaction of the Post Graduate teachers on handling primary classes. At the same time they may be well aware of some of the items that were stressed in the training programmes. Now a days many highly quailed people are choosing teaching profession by chance. The main reasons for this are the availability of government jobs in teaching field. Some of the highly qualified people are aiming to get higher posts using this job as a time pass activity. Then naturally they may not show as much interest and aptitude in this job. Teachers who enter the profession with B.Ed. or M.Ed. do not possess the requisite teaching aptitude for teaching children of primary classes. In the case of students with D.Ed. methodology, there is scope for teaching all the five subjects that were learnt in their D.Ed. course. Naturally, they may be interested in teaching and show positive attitude towards attending the training programmes. Teaching of primary classes mainly requires teaching skill. Methodology is more important than content depth for effective teaching in primary classes. Therefore focus is to be given on methodology orientation rather than content transaction. Activity oriented training programmes are to be planned. Even highly qualified teachers may not be aware of the primary school methodology. In the discussions that take place as part of training programme, teachers with higher qualifications should be involved actively.

7. *Both the categories of primary teachers, having 15 years or less experience and above 15 years of experience are having high attitude towards the effectiveness of in-service training programmes without any significant difference*

Generally, teachers having more experience may be aware of all the classroom methodologies. There fore, there is chance for not showing interest towards training programmes. As service increases, as also increases. This may be a problem for their disinterest towards training programmes. It is a happy sign to note that irrespective of age and experience, all teachers have shown high attitude towards training programmes. This is a good sign in the positive direction. It is to be noted that learning is a continuous process and at the same time new methodology evolves year by year. Therefore a teacher has to be equipped with the latest knowledge that is emerging in the field. In order to develop the attitude of more experienced teachers, their services are to be utilized as resource persons etc., They should be provided opportunity to share their experiences in the teaching field with young teachers. So, training programmes are to be designed in such a manner that would equally develop interest and attitude among the senior teachers. Training methods should not be in lecture method but should be in participatory mode. Modules should be supplied in advance so that teachers go through them and attend with some readiness. These things will be helpful in making the training programmes an effective one. If training programmes are arranged in summer vacation, air coolers, cool water are must to ensure the effectiveness of the programmes.

Regarding conduct of training programmes, teachers raised certain issues on quality of input given by resource persons providing minimum facilities such as good accommodation with fans, water facility, supply of course material etc., This needs to be given priority by the department. For that, a good accommodation with fans and water facility is to be chosen as the venue of training programmes.

To raise the quality of the programmes, resource persons to be selected from DIETS and B.Ed. colleges. Also at least certain part of the training programme is to be through tele-mode and video conferencing so that the quality of the programmes is not diluted. Also course material is to be supplied to teachers in advance so that they attend the programmes with some understanding and active interaction will take place during the course of training.

SUGGESTIONS FOR FURTHER RESEARCH

As this is a small piece of study limited to 150 P.S. teachers, the researcher makes the following suggestions for further study on a broader sample.

It is only a small piece of study involving limited teachers at the Primary level, and therefore a more intensive study may be taken up at various levels of schooling across the State.

A more detailed study regarding "the Impact of teacher trainings on learner, teacher, and parents" may be undertaken.

Studies may be conducted on theme-wise in-service teacher trainings at various levels detail.

A study may be conducted on the views of teachers, inspecting authorities, resource persons at the training centres, (DIETS) parents, learners and other community members on the in-service teachers' trainings in view of reformation of the Primary school system.

There is need to study on the physical facilities provided at the venue of the training programmes.

There is need to study on the resourcefulness of State Resource Persons and District Resource Persons.

There is need to study on the timing of the training programmes.

There is need to study whether the needs and suggestions of the participants are taken into consideration while planning the training programmes.

There is need to study on the course material or, modules to be given to the trainees.

There is need to study on the problems faced by the lady teachers in attending the training programmes.

There is need to study on the effectiveness of training programmes in relation to other variables like promotion to the next higher grade.

There is need to study on the in-service training programmes through tele-conferencing mode.

There is need to study on the implementation of training received, in the classroom teaching.

There is need to study on the effectiveness of innovative programmes that are implemented in schools.

Bibliography

"Action Researches and Innovative Practices" An IGNOU-MHRD Government of India Project, March, 2005.

Anastasi, A. (1982), Psychological Testing, (5th edition, (New York): Appleton Lentory Crafts.

Bhaskar Rao, Digumarti (1998), District Primary Educational Programme, New Delhi: Discovery Publishing House.

Budholia, O.P. (2002),"Universalization of Elementary Education: A Challenge for the Third Millennium". Miracle of Teaching, Volume-2, No. 2.

Carthel J.T. (1977). An Analysis of Document Reported in Selected In-service Programmes. Unpublished paper of University of Texas, Austin Texas.

DEP-SSA (2006), Handbook on Continuous and Comprehensive Evaluation. Distance Education Programme-Sarva Siksha Abhiyan, IGNOU, New Delhi.

Delors, Jacques (1996) Learning: The Treasure Within: Report to UNESCO of the International Commission Education for the Twentyfirst Century: UNESCO.

"DPEP Calling", March, 1999, Newsletter from Department of Education, MHRD, New Delhi.

'DPEP Calling', Jan-Mar 2002, a DPEP Newsletter of Department of Elementary Education &Literacy, MHRD, Shastri Bhavan, New Delhi.

"Education and National Development Report" of the Education Commission, 1964-66, First Edition, Vol.1, NCERT Publication, 1966.

"Elementary Teacher Education" A Blueprint of Process Management, NCERT, 2003.

"Envisioning Teacher Education" in the 10th Plan and Beyond, NCERT, New Delhi, 2003.

Engelking, Jeri L. (1987), "Attracting and Retaining Quality Teachers through Incentives". NASSPL Bulletin 1-6.

Fifth Survey of Educational Research 1988-1992, NCERT, New Delhi.

Fullan, M (1982), The Meaning of Educational Change. New York: Teachers College Press.

Garrett, H.E. (2005): Statistics in Psychology and Education, Paragon International Publishers, New Delhi.

Global Movement for Children (1990) "Convention on the Rights of the Child", World Summit for Children, New York.

Good, C.V. (1972), Essentials of Educational Research Methodology and Design, New York: Appleton Lentory Crafts.

Govinda, R. (2003), Providing Elementary Education for All: Challenges to Teacher Education.

Handbook of Research for Educational Communications and Technology (1996): Macmillan Library Reference USA, Simon and Macmillan, New York.

"Innovation and Evaluation Strategies for Quality Elementary Education", Distance Education Programme — Sarva Shiksha Abhiyan, IGNOU, 2007.

International Bureau of Education (1985), 'In-service Teacher Education'. Bulletin of the International Bureau of Education, 234, 7-103 and 235, 204-206.

Jangira, N.K., Yadav, D.D. (1994). "District Primary Education Programme — Baseline Assessment Study of Four Districts of Assam," NCERT, New Delhi: (Mimeo).

Jangira, N.K., Singh A. and Garg, VP (1994), District Primary Education Programme. "Workshop on Training Needs of Teachers", NCERT, Now Delhi (Mimeo).

Journal of All India Association for Educational Research, Volume-13, March-June 2001, Volume 18, Sept-Dec; 2006.

K.S.N. Raju (2008), "A Study on the Impact of Trainings given to In-service Teachers in Khammam District".

Mama, K., Bombay University 1980, "A Study of the Impact of In-service Education on the Teachers in the State of Maharashtra".

MHRD-NIEPA (2000): Education for All: India, New Delhi, And MHRD-NIEPA Publication.

National Policy on Education Revised in 1992, New Delhi, Department of Education (1996).

National Curriculum Framework, 2005 Chairman: Prof. Yashpal.

NCERT (2003), Action Research, Handbook for Primary Teachers. National Council of Educational Research and Training, New Delhi.

NCERT (2003), Continuous and Comprehensive Evaluation, Teachers Handbook for Primary Stage. National Council of Educational Research and Training, New Delhi.

NCERT (2002), The Primary Teacher Volume. xxvii No. 3, New Delhi: NCERT.

NCTE (2004), Some Specific Issues and Concerns of Teacher Education. National Council of Teacher Education, New Delhi.

Ruth, K.K (2002), "Retaining Children in Schools Through Play Way and Activity Based Methods". Primary Teacher, Vol. 27, No. 3.

"Research Trends in Staff Development and In- service Education". Journal of Education for Teaching (1987), 13(1), 3-1.

Robert V. Bullough "The Continuing Education of Teachers: In-service Training and Workshops" Springer International Hand Tools of Education, 2009, Volume 21, 3, 159-169.

Report of the Working Group on Elementary and Adult Education, Tenth Five Year Plan 2002-2007 (2001), New Delhi, Department of Elementary Education and Literacy.

Report of the Education Commission, 1964-66, Vol. 1, NCERT Publication First Edition, 1966.

S. Ratna Kumari (2008), "Evaluation of Impact of Trainings Given by DIETs to In-service Teachers".

SCERT, Andhra Pradesh (1987), "Evaluation of In-service Training Programme for Primary Teachers in the Selected Government and Aided Teacher Training Institutions".

Shukla, Shraddha (2003), "Strengthening Primary Education: The Heart of the System", Miracle of Teaching, Vol. 3, No. 2.

Sixth All India Survey (1998), New Delhi, NCERT. 17. (2000) 44. Sarva Siksha Abhiyan: A Programme for Universal Elementary Education, A Framework for Implementation, New Delhi, Department of Elementary Education and Literacy.

Selected Educational Statistics (2002), New Delhi, Department of Secondary and Higher Education (2000-2001).

Sparks, Dand Loncks, Horsley (1990) Models of Staff Development in W.R.Houston (Ed) Handbook of Research on Teachers Education, New York: Macmillan.

Sethumadhavan and Jayachandran, Madhubala (2007), A Study on Impact of Distance Education Activities Undertaken by DEP-DPEP.

Shukla, S. et. al. (1993), A Study of Attainment of Primary School Students in Various States, DMESDP, NCERT, New Delhi.

Sharma, Subhash Chandra (1992), 'A Critical Study of the Impact of In-service Education on the Professional Efficiency of Teachers of PGT Scale Working in Kendriya Vidyalayas of Lucknow Region'.

Third Survey of Educational Research in 1978-1983, NCERT.

The Yashpal Committee Report on "Learning Without Burden".

Teleconferencing and Training Kit (2005): Commonwealth Educational Media Centre for Asia.

UNICEF (1999), The State of the World's Children, New York: UNICEF, 29.

Vyas, J.C. (1991), A study on 'Effectiveness of Performance of Teachers Trained Under the Programme of Mass Orientation of School Teachers'.

Wolfenshon, James D. (2000), A Time for Action: Placing Education at the Core of Development.

"World Declaration on Education for All and Framework for Action to Meet Basic Learning Needs" Adopted by the 'World Conference on Education for All — Meeting Basic Learning Needs', Jomtien, Thailand 5-9 March, 1990.

Additional Reading

Bhaskara Rao, Digumarti (1994). *Scientific Aptitude*. New Delhi: Ashish Publishing House. ISBN 81-7024-658-X.

Bhaskara Rao, Digumarti (1995). *Animal Kingdom*. New Delhi: Discovery Publishing House. ISBN 81-7141-274-2.

Bhaskara Rao, Digumarti (1995). *Batracology*. New Delhi: Discovery Publishing House. ISBN 81-7141-279-3.

Bhaskara Rao, Digumarti (1997). *Scientific Attitude*. New Delhi: Discovery Publishing House. ISBN 81-7141-381-1.

Bhaskara Rao, Digumarti (1996). *Scientific Attitude vis-à-vis Scientific Aptitude*. New Delhi: Discovery Publishing House. ISBN 81-7141-308-0.

Bhaskara Rao, Digumarti (2004). *Scientific Attitude, Scientific Aptitude and Achievement*. New Delhi: Discovery Publishing House. ISBN 81-7141-781-7.

Bhaskara Rao, Digumarti (2004). *Educational Administration*. New Delhi: Discovery Publishing House. ISBN 81-7141-842-2.

Bhaskara Rao, Digumarti (2004). *Issues in School Education*. New Delhi: Discovery Publishing House. ISBN 81-8356-025-3.

Bhaskara Rao, Digumarti, Editor (1996). *Encyclopaedia of Education For All*, 5 volumes. New Delhi: APH Publishing Corporation. ISBN 81-7024-759-4 (set).

- *Vol. I* *Education For All: The World Conference*. ISBN 81-7024-760-8.
- *Vol. II* *Education For All: The EPA-9 Summit*. ISBN 81-7024-761-6.
- *Vol. II* *Education For All: Quality Education For All*. ISBN 81-7024-762-6.
- *Vol. IV* *Education For All: Planning and Monitoring*. ISBN 81-7024-763-4.
- *Vol. V* *Education For All: The Indian Scenario*. ISBN 81-7024-764-0.

Bhaskara Rao, Digumarti, Editor (1999). *International Encyclopaedia of AIDS*, 11 volumes. New Delhi: Discovery Publishing House. ISBN 81-7141-522-6 (set).

- *Vol. 1* *Introduction to HIV/AIDS*. ISBN 81-7141-523-7.
- *Vol. 2* *HIV/AIDS – Issues and Challenges,* 2 parts. ISBN 81-7141-524-5.
- *Vol. 3* *HIV/AIDS – Socio Economic Realities*. ISBN 81-7141-524-3.

Vol. 4 *HIV/AIDS – Law Ethics and Human Rights,* 2 parts. ISBN 81-7141-526-1.

Vol. 5 *AIDS and NGOs.* ISBN 81-7141-527-X.

Vol. 6 *AIDS and Home Care.* ISBN 81-7141-528-8.

Vol. 7. *STD Case Management.* ISBN 81-7141-529-6.

Vol. 8 *HIV/AIDS Prevention and Care — Teaching Modules for Nurses and Midwives.* ISBN 81-7141-530-X.

Vol. 9 *HIV Prevention Education for Educational Institutions.* ISBN 81-7141-531-8.

Vol. 10 *Instructional Modules for AIDS Education.* ISBN 81-7141-532-6.

Vol. 11 *School Health Education to Prevent AIDS and STD — A Package for Curriculum Planners.* ISBN 81-7141-533-4.

Bhaskara Rao, Digumarti, Editor (2000). *International Encyclopaedia of Human Rights,* 7 volumes in 13 parts. New Delhi: Discovery Publishing House. ISBN 81-7141-567-9 (set).

Vol. 1 *International Instruments of Human Rights,* 2 parts. ISBN 81-7141-569-4.

Vol. 2 *Regional Instruments of Human Rights.* ISBN 81-7141-604-7.

Vol. 3 *Human Rights and the United Nations,* 2 parts. ISBN 81-7141-605-5.

Vol. 4 *Fact Files of Human Rights,* 3 parts. ISBN 81-7141-606-3.

Vol. 5 *Study Stories of Human Rights,* 3 parts. ISBN 81-7141-607-3.

Vol. 6 *International Meetings on Human Rights,* 2 parts. ISBN 81-714-608-X.

Vol. 7 *Professional Training in Human Rights.* ISBN 81-7141-609-8.

Bhaskara Rao, Digumarti, Editor (2000). *International Encyclopaedia of Science and Technology Education*, 11 volumes. New Delhi: Discovery Publishing House. ISBN 81-7141-548-2 (set).

Vol. 1 *Science and Technology Education*. ISBN 81-7141-568-7.

Vol. 2 *Science Education in Developing Countries*. ISBN 81-7141-569-9.

Vol. 3 *Organizational Structure of Science*. ISBN 81-7141-570-9.

Vol. 4 *Science Education in Asia and the Pacific*. ISBN 81-7141-571-7

Vol. 5 *Science and Technology Education For All*. ISBN 81-7141-572-5.

Vol. 6 *Values, Ethics, Talent and Girls in Science and Technology Education*. ISBN 81-7141-573-3.

Vol. 7 *Popularization of Science and Technology Education*. ISBN 81-7141-574-1.

Vol. 8 *Science, Power and Society*. ISBN 81-7141- 575-X.

Vol. 9 *Information Technology*. ISBN 81-7141-576-8.

Vol. 10 *Teacher Training in Science and Technology Education*. ISBN 81-7142-577-6.

Vol. 11 *Teacher Training in Science and Technology: A Curriculum Framework*. ISBN 81-7141-578-4.

Bhaskara Rao, Digumarti, Editor (2000). *Education For All: Achieving the Goal*, 3 volumes. New Delhi: APH Publishing Corporation. ISBN 81-7648-152-1 (set).

Vol. I *The Global Consensus*. ISBN 81-7648-155-6.

Vol. II *Mid-Decade Review Reports of Regional Seminars*. ISBN 81-7648-154-8.

Vol. III *Issues and Trends*. ISBN 81-7648-155-6.

Bhaskara Rao, Digumarti, Editor (2004). *International Encyclopaedia of Learning to Live Together,* 4 Volumes. New Delhi: Discovery Publishing House. ISBN 81-7141-848-1.

Vol. 1 International Conference on Learning to Live Together.

Vol. 2 Globalization and Living Together.

Vol. 3 Curriculum for Learning to Live Together.

Vol. 4 Science Education for the Contemporary Society.

Bhaskara Rao, Digumarti, Editor (2005). *Encyclopaedia of Education For All,* 3 Volumes. New Delhi: Discovery Publishing House. ISBN 81-7141-647-0 (set).

Bhaskara Rao, Digumarti, Editor (2007). *Encyclopaedia of Teacher Education,* 4 Volumes. New Delhi: Discovery Publishing House. ISBN 81-8356-306-6 (set).

Bhaskara Rao, Digumarti, Editor (2007). *Encyclopaedia of Edeucation for Living Together,* 4 Volumes. New Delhi: Discovery Publishing House. ISBN 81-7141-848-1 (set).

Bhaskara Rao, Digumarti, Editor (1996). *National Policy on Education,* 2 Volumes. New Delhi: Anmol Publications Pvt. Ltd. ISBN 81-7488-323-1.

Bhaskara Rao, Digumarti, Editor (1996). *Global Perceptions on Peace Education,* 3 Volumes. New Delhi: Discovery Publishing House. ISBN 81-7141-319-6.

Bhaskara Rao, Digumarti, Editor (1997). *Education for the 21st Century*. New Delhi: Discovery Publishing House. ISBN 81-7141-389-7.

Bhaskara Rao, Digumarti, Editor (1997). *Reflections on Scientific Attitude*. New Delhi: Discovery Publishing House. ISBN 81-7141-319-6.

Bhaskara Rao, Digumarti, Editor (1997). *Success Story of a Primary Education Project*. New Delhi: APH Publishing Corporation. ISBN 81-7024-850-7.

Bhaskara Rao, Digumarti, Editor (1997). *World Food Summit*. New Delhi: Discovery Publishing House. ISBN 81-7141-386-2.

Bhaskara Rao, Digumarti, Editor (1997). *Care the Child,* 2 Volumes. New Delhi: Discovery Publishing House. ISBN 81-7141-394-3.

Bhaskara Rao, Digumarti, Editor (1998). *Earth Summit,* 2 Volumes. New Delhi: Discovery Publishing House. ISBN 81-7141-435-4.

Bhaskara Rao, Digumarti, Editor (1998). *Adolescence Education*. New Delhi: Discovery Publishing House. ISBN 81-7141-432-X.

Bhaskara Rao, Digumarti, Editor (1998). *Community and School Nutrition Education*. New Delhi: Discovery Publishing House. ISBN 81-7141-435-4.

Bhaskara Rao, Digumarti, Editor (1998). *District Primary Education Programme*. New Delhi: Discovery Publishing House. ISBN 81-7141-396-X.

Bhaskara Rao, Digumarti, Editor (1998). *National Policy on Education: Towards an Enlightened and Humane Society*. New Delhi: Discovery Publishing House. ISBN 81-7141-426-5.

Bhaskara Rao, Digumarti, Editor (1998). *Reforming School Education*. New Delhi: Discovery Publishing House. ISBN 81-7141-403-6.

Bhaskara Rao, Digumarti, Editor (1998). *Teacher Education in India*. New Delhi: Discovery Publishing House. ISBN 81-7141-406-0.

Bhaskara Rao, Digumarti, Editor (1998). *World Summit for Social Development*. New Delhi: Discovery Publishing House. ISBN 81-7141-420-6.

Bhaskara Rao, Digumarti, Editor (2001). *Nuclear Materials: Issues and Concerns*, 2 Volumes. New Delhi: Discovery Publishing House. ISBN 81-7141-611-X.

Bhaskara Rao, Digumarti, Editor (2001). *Distance Education in Different Countries*. New Delhi: APH Publishing Corporation. ISBN 81-7648-229-3.

Bhaskara Rao, Digumarti, Editor (2001). *Decentralised Management of Education: Management of Education in Panchayati Raj and Municipal Bodies*. New Delhi: Discovery Publishing House. ISBN 81-7141-617-9.

Bhaskara Rao, Digumarti, Editor (2001). *Electrochemistry for Environmental Protection*. New Delhi: Discovery Publishing House. ISBN 81-7141-619-5.

Bhaskara Rao, Digumarti, Editor (2001). *Global Educational Studies*. New Delhi: Discovery Publishing House. ISBN 81-7141-616-0.

Bhaskara Rao, Digumarti, Editor (2001). *Global Synthesis of Educational Assessment*. New Delhi: Discovery Publishing House. ISBN 81-7141-613-6.

Bhaskara Rao, Digumarti, Editor (2001). *Jomtein Decade of Education*. New Delhi: Discovery Publishing House. ISBN 81-7141-618-7.

Bhaskara Rao, Digumarti, Editor (2001). *World Conference on Education for All*. New Delhi: APH Publishing House.

Bhaskara Rao, Digumarti, Editor (2001). *World Conference on Higher Education*. New Delhi: Discovery Publishing House. ISBN 81-7141-610-1.

Bhaskara Rao, Digumarti, Editor (2001). *World Conference on Science*. New Delhi: Discovery Publishing House. ISBN 81-7141-612-8.

Bhaskara Rao, Digumarti, Editor (2003). *Inspiring Experiences in Teacher Education*. New Delhi: Discovery Publishing House. ISBN 81-7141-656-X.

Bhaskara Rao, Digumarti, Editor (2003). *International Studies in Education*, 3 Volumes. New Delhi: Discovery Publishing House. ISBN 81-7141-647-0.

Bhaskara Rao, Digumarti, Editor (2003). *Military Conversion: Impact on Science and Technology*. New Delhi: Discovery Publishing House. ISBN 81-7141-578-4.

Bhaskara Rao, Digumarti, Editor (2003). *United Nations Millennium Summit*. New Delhi: Discovery Publishing House. ISBN 81-7141-632-2.

Bhaskara Rao, Digumarti, Editor (2003). *World Assembly on Aging*. New Delhi: Discovery Publishing House. ISBN 81-7141-637-3.

Bhaskara Rao, Digumarti, Editor (2003). *World Conference on Human Rights*. New Delhi: Discovery Publishing House. ISBN 81-7141-661-6.

Bhaskara Rao, Digumarti, Editor (2003). *World Education Forum*. New Delhi: Discovery Publishing House. ISBN 81-7141-639-X.

Bhaskara Rao, Digumarti, Editor (2003). *Education, Employment and Human Resource Development*. New Delhi: Discovery Publishing House. ISBN 81-7141- 681-0.

Bhaskara Rao, Digumarti, Editor (2003). *Successful Schooling*. New Delhi: Discovery Publishing House. ISBN 81-7141-677-2.

Bhaskara Rao, Digumarti, Editor (2003). *European Education and Teachers*. New Delhi: Discovery Publishing House. ISBN 81-7141-702-7.

Bhaskara Rao, Digumarti, Editor (2003). *Teachers in a Changing World*. New Delhi: Discovery Publishing House. ISBN 81-7141-694-2.

Bhaskara Rao, Digumarti, Editor (2004). *International Guidelines on Open and Distance Teacher Education*. New Delhi: Discovery Publishing House. ISBN 81-7141-777-9.

Bhaskara Rao, Digumarti, Editor (2004). *Adult Learning in the 21st Century*. New Delhi: Discovery Publishing House. ISBN 81-7141-797-3.

Bhaskara Rao, Digumarti, Editor (2004). *Educational Practices: Research and Recommendations*. New Delhi: Discovery Publishing House. ISBN 81-7141-835-X.

Bhaskara Rao, Digumarti, Editor (2004). *General Secondary Education In the 21st Century*. New Delhi: Discovery Publishing House.

Bhaskara Rao, Digumarti, Editor (2004). *Reforming Secondary Education*. New Delhi: Discovery Publishing House. ISBN 81-7141-843-0.

Bhaskara Rao, Digumarti, Editor (2004). *Human Rights Education*. New Delhi: Discovery Publishing House. ISBN 81-7141-882-1.

Bhaskara Rao, Digumarti, Editor (2004). *United Nations Decade for Human Rights Education*. New Delhi: Discovery Publishing House. ISBN 81-7141- 887-2.

Bhaskara Rao, Digumarti, Editor (2004). *Technical and Vocational Education and Training in the 21st Century*. New Delhi: Discovery Publishing House. ISBN 81-7141-984-4.

Bhaskara Rao, Digumarti, Editor (2005). *Encyclopaedia of Education For All*, 3 Volumes. New Delhi: Discovery Publishing House.

Bhaskara Rao, Digumarti, Editor (2011). *Right to Education*. Hyderabad: Neel Kamal Publishers.

Bhaskara Rao, Digumarti, Editor (2011). *International Encyclopaedia of Educational Policies*. Hyderabad: Neel Kamal Publishers.

Bhaskara Rao, Digumarti, Editor (2011). *International Encyclopaedia of Educational Practices*. Hyderabad: Neel Kamal Publishers.

Bhaskara Rao, Digumarti and B.S.V. Dutt, Editors (2003). *Education: Programmes and Policies*. New Delhi: APH Publishing House. ISBN 81-7648-470-9.

Bhaskara Rao, Digumarti, C.A.P. Swamy and B.S.V. Dutt (1997). *Self-Evaluation in Student Teaching*. New Delhi: Discovery Publishing House. ISBN 81-7141-374-9.

Bhaskara Rao, Digumarti and C. D. Swarna Lattha, Editors (2006). *Encyclopaedia of Biotechnology,* 5 Volumes. New Delhi: Discovery Publishing House. ISBN 81-8356-168-3 (set).

Bhaskara Rao, Digumarti, C. Sridevi and K. Vijaya (1995). *Achievement in Social Studies*. New Delhi: Discovery Publishing House. ISBN 81-7141-281-5.

Bhaskara Rao, Digumarti and D. Naresh Kumar (2004). *School Teacher Effectiveness*. New Delhi: Discovery Publishing House. ISBN 81-7141-782-5.

Bhaskara Rao, Digumarti and D. Sridhar (2002). *Job Satisfaction of School Teachers*. New Delhi: Discovery Publishing House. ISBN 81-7141-652-7.

Bhaskara Rao, Digumarti and Digumarti Pushpa Latha, Editors (1998). *International Encyclopaedia of Women,* 5 volumes. New Delhi: Discovery Publishing House. ISBN 81-7141-410-9 (set).

Vol. 1 *Status of World's Women*. ISBN 81-7141- 494-X.

Vol. 2 *Women, Education and Empowerment*. ISBN 81-7141-498-1.

Vol. 3 *Women Challenges and Advancement*. ISBN 81-7141-497-4.

Vol. 4 *Women and Family Health*. ISBN 81-7141-497-4.

Vol. 5 *Women and International Action*. ISBN 81-7141-498-2.

Bhaskara Rao, Digumarti and Digumarti Pushpa Latha (1994). *Achievement in Biology*. New Delhi: Discovery Publishing House. ISBN 81-7141-264-5.

Bhaskara Rao, Digumarti and Digumarti Pushpa Latha (1995). *Achievement in English*. New Delhi: Discovery Publishing House. ISBN 81-7141-283-1.

Bhaskara Rao, Digumarti and Digumarti Pushpa Latha (1994). *Achievement in Science*. New Delhi: Discovery Publishing House. ISBN 81-7141-280-70.

Bhaskara Rao, Digumarti and Digumarti Pushpa Latha (1995). *Achievement in Mathematics*. New Delhi: Discovery Publishing House. ISBN 81-7141-278-5.

Bhaskara Rao, Digumarti and Digumarti Pushpa Latha (2004). *Education for Women*. New Delhi: Discovery Publishing House. ISBN 81-7141-873-2.

Bhaskara Rao, Digumarti, Digumarti Pushpa Latha and Digumarthi Harshitha, Editors (2001). *Biological Warfare*. New Delhi: Discovery Publishing House. ISBN 81-7141-597-0.

Bhaskara Rao, Digumarti, Digumarti Pushpa Latha and Digumarthi Harshitha, Editors (2001). *Women as Educators*. New Delhi: Discovery Publishing House. ISBN 81-7141-602-0.

Bhaskara Rao, Digumarti and Digumarthi Harshitha (2004). *Adjustment of Adolescents*. New Delhi: APH Publishing House. ISBN 81-7648-836-8.

Bhaskara Rao, Digumarti and Digumarthi Harshitha, Editors (2001). *Education in India*. New Delhi: APH Publishing House. ISBN 81-7648-207-2.

Bhaskara Rao, Digumarti, Digumarti Pushpa Latha and Digumarthi Harshitha, Editors (2001). *Assessing Learning Achievement*. New Delhi: Discovery Publishing House. ISBN 81-7141-601-2.

Bhaskara Rao, Digumarti, Digumarti Pushpa Latha and Digumarthi Harshitha, Editors (2001). *Energy Security*. New Delhi: Discovery Publishing House. ISBN 81-7141-598-9.

Bhaskara Rao, Digumarti, Digumarthi Harshitha and K.R.S. Sambasiva Rao, Editors (1999). *Advanced Biotechnology*. New Delhi: Discovery Publishing House. ISBN 81-7141-516-4.

Bhaskara Rao, Digumarti and K.R.S. Sambasiva Rao, Editors (1996). *Current Trends in Indian Education*. New Delhi: Discovery Publishing House. ISBN 81-7141-311-0.

Bhaskara Rao, Digumarti and D. Naresh Kumar (2004). *School Teacher Effectiveness*. New Delhi: Discovery Publishing House. ISBN 81-7141-782-5.

Bhaskara Rao, Digumarti and E. Sreekanth Babu (2004). *Educational Interests of School Students*. New Delhi: Discovery Publishing House. ISBN 81-7141-837-6.

Bhaskara Rao, Digumarti and K. Vijaya (1995). *A Text Book Evaluation*. Ambala Cantt: The Associated Publishers.

Bhaskara Rao, Digumarti and M.A. Fayaz (2004). *Problems of Primary School Drop-outs*. New Delhi: Discovery Publishing House. ISBN 81-7141-834-1.

Bhaskara Rao, Digumarti and N.V.M. Mohana Rao (2002). *Problems of Mentally Handicapped Children*. New Delhi: Discovery Publishing House. ISBN 81-7141-645-4.

Bhaskara Rao, Digumarti and S. Chandra Mohan (2002). *Sports Management*. New Delhi: APH Publishing House. ISBN 81-7648-467-9.

Bhaskara Rao, Digumarti and S.A. Khader (2004). *Problems of Private School Teachers*. New Delhi: Discovery Publishing Corporation. ISBN 81-7141-838-4.

Bhaskara Rao, Digumarti and S.A. Khader (2004). *School Education in India*. New Delhi: Discovery Publishing Corporation. ISBN 81-7141-849-X.

Bhaskara Rao, Digumarti and Sk. Johni Basha (2004). *Teachers' Population Education Awareness*. New Delhi: Discovery Publishing House. ISBN 81-7141-832-5.

Bhaskara Rao, Digumarti, V.V. Rao, V.V. Lakshmi and V.V. Krishna, Editors (1999). *Status and Advancement of Women*. New Delhi: APH Publishing Corporation. ISBN 81-7648-169-6.

Appala Naidu, P.Ch., Author and Digumarti Bhaskara Rao, Editor (2007). *Feedback Methods and Student Performance*. New Delhi: Discovery Publishing House. ISBN 81-8356-284-1.

Babu, P.C., Author and Digumarti Bhaskara Rao, Editor (2004). *Flowers of Wisdom*. New Delhi: Discovery Publishing House. ISBN 81-7141-695-0.

Bujji Babu, K., Author and Digumarti Bhaskara Rao, Editor (2007). *Teaching Aptitude of Primary School Teachers*. New Delhi: Sonali Publications. ISBN 81-8411-083-9.

Amala, P. A. and Anupama, P., Authors and Digumarti Bhaskara Rao, Editor (2004). *History of Education*. New Delhi: Discovery Publishing House. ISBN 81-7141-860-0.

Bhagya Lakshmi, L., Author and Digumarti Bhaskara Rao, Editor (2000). *Reading and Comprehension*. New Delhi: Discovery Publishing House. ISBN 81-7141-543-1.

Bhasha, S.A., Author and Digumarti Bhaskara Rao, Editor (2004). *Methods of Teaching Geography*. New Delhi: Discovery Publishing House. ISBN 81-7141-807-4.

Bhuvaneswara Lakshmi, Gadde, Author and Digumarti Bhaskara Rao, Editor(2000). *Attitude Towards Science*. New Delhi: Discovery Publishing House. ISBN 81-7141-541-6.

Bhuvaneswara Lakshmi, G., Author and Digumarti Bhaskara Rao, Editor (2004). *Methods of Teaching Life Science*. New Delhi: Discovery Publishing House. ISBN 81-7141-804-X.

Bhuvaneswara Lakshmi, G. and K. Subba Rao, Authors and Digumarti Bhaskara Rao, Editor (2004). *Methods of Teaching Biology*. New Delhi: Discovery Publishing House. ISBN 81-7141-914-3.

Chary, K.V.N.B., Author and Digumarti Bhaskara Rao, Editor (2006). *Techniques of Teaching Physics*. New Delhi: Sonali Publications. ISBN 81-8411-046-4.

Chowdary, S.B.J.R. and Naga Raju, Authors and Digumarti Bhaskara Rao, Editor (2004). *Mastery of Teaching Skills*. New Delhi: Discovery Publishing House. ISBN 81-7141-861-9.

Dayakara Reddy, V. and Digumarti Bhaskara Rao, Editors (2006). *Value-oriented Education*. New Delhi: Discovery Publishing House. ISBN 81-8356-051-2.

Devraj, T.A.S., Author and Digumarti Bhaskara Rao, Editor (1997). *Trace Analysis of Uranium and Thorium*. New Delhi: Discovery Publishing House. ISBN 81-7141-375-7.

Durga Rani, K., Author and Digumarti Bhaskara Rao, Editor (2000). *Educational Aspirations and Scientific Attitudes*. New Delhi: Discovery Publishing House. ISBN 81-7141-555-5.

Dutt, B.S.V. and Digumarti Bhaskara Rao (2001). *Empowering Primary Teachers*. New Delhi: Discovery Publishing House. ISBN 81-7141-615-2.

Dutt, B.S.V., Author and Digumarti Bhaskara Rao, Editor (2004). *Comparative Education*. New Delhi: Discovery Publishing House. ISBN 81-7141-912-7.

Ediger, Marlow and Digumarti Bhaskara Rao, Editors (2006). *Encyclopaedia of School Education*, 5 Volumes. New Delhi: Discovery Publishing House. ISBN 81-8356-308-2 (set).

Ediger, Marlow and Digumarti Bhaskara Rao, Editors (2006). *Encyclopaedia of School Administration*, 4 Volumes. New Delhi: Discovery Publishing House. ISBN 81-8356-307-4 (set).

Ediger, Marlow and Digumarti Bhaskara Rao, Editors (2007). *Encyclopaedia of School Curriculum*, 10 Volumes. New Delhi: Discovery Publishing House. ISBN 81-8356-305-8 (set).

Ediger, Marlow and Digumarti Bhaskara Rao, Editors (2007). *Encyclopaedia of Teaching*, 8 Volumes. New Delhi: Discovery Publishing House. ISBN 81-8356-305-8 (set).

Marlow Ediger and Digumarti Bhaskara Rao, Editors (2006). *Encyclopaedia of School Education*, 5 Volumes. New Delhi: Discovery Publishing House. ISBN 81-8356-308-2 (set).

Marlow Ediger and Digumarti Bhaskara Rao, Editors (2006). *Encyclopaedia of School Administration*, 4 Volumes. New Delhi: Discovery Publishing House. ISBN 81-8356-307-4 (set).

Marlow Ediger and Digumarti Bhaskara Rao, Editors (2007). *Encyclopaedia of School Curriculum,* 10 Volumes. New Delhi: Discovery Publishing House. ISBN 81-8356-305-8 (set).

Marlow Ediger and Digumarti Bhaskara Rao, Editors (2007). *Encyclopaedia of Teaching,* 8 Volumes. New Delhi: Discovery Publishing House. ISBN 81-8356-305-8 (set).

Ediger, Marlow and Digumarti Bhaskara Rao (1996). *Science Curriculum*. New Delhi: Discovery Publishing House. ISBN 81-7141-321-8.

Ediger, Marlow and Digumarti Bhaskara Rao (2000). *Teaching Mathematics Successfully*. New Delhi: Discovery Publishing House. ISBN 81-7141-552-0.

Ediger, Marlow and Digumarti Bhaskara Rao (2001). *Teaching Science Successfully*. New Delhi: Discovery Publishing House. ISBN 81-7141-600-4.

Ediger, Marlow and Digumarti Bhaskara Rao (2001). *Teaching Social Studies Successfully*. New Delhi: Discovery Publishing House. ISBN 81-7141-596-2.

Ediger, Marlow and Digumarti Bhaskara Rao (2002). *Philosophy and Curriculum*. New Delhi: Discovery Publishing House. ISBN 81-7141-631-4.

Ediger, Marlow and Digumarti Bhaskara Rao (2002). *Improving School Administration*. New Delhi: Discovery Publishing House. ISBN 81-7141-633-0

Ediger, Marlow and Digumarti Bhaskara Rao (2002). *Elementary Curriculum*. New Delhi: Discovery Publishing House. ISBN 81-7141-658-6.

Ediger, Marlow and Digumarti Bhaskara Rao (2003). *Language Arts Curriculum*. New Delhi: Discovery Publishing House. ISBN 81-7141-657-8.

Ediger, Marlow and Digumarti Bhaskara Rao (2003). *Psychology and Curriculum*. New Delhi: Discovery Publishing House. ISBN 81-7141-691-8.

Ediger, Marlow and Digumarti Bhaskara Rao (2003). *Teaching Language Arts Successfully*. New Delhi: Discovery Publishing House. ISBN 81-7141-678-0.

Ediger, Marlow and Digumarti Bhaskara Rao (2003). *School Curriculum and Administration*. New Delhi: Discovery Publishing House. ISBN 81-7141-709-4.

Ediger, Marlow and Digumarti Bhaskara Rao (2003). *Teaching Mathematics in Elementary Schools*. New Delhi: Discovery Publishing House. ISBN 81-7141-687-X.

Ediger, Marlow and Digumarti Bhaskara Rao (2003). *Teaching Science in Elementary Schools*. New Delhi: Discovery Publishing House. ISBN 81-7141-698-5.

Ediger, Marlow and Digumarti Bhaskara Rao (2003). *School Curriculum and Administration*. New Delhi: Discovery Publishing House. ISBN 81-7141-709-4.

Ediger, Marlow and Digumarti Bhaskara Rao (2003). *Elementary Curriculum Improvement*. New Delhi: Discovery Publishing House. ISBN 81-7141-740-X.

Ediger, Marlow and Digumarti Bhaskara Rao (2004). *School Organisation*. New Delhi: Discovery Publishing House. ISBN 81-7141-843-0.

Ediger, Marlow and Digumarti Bhaskara Rao (2004). *Relevancy in Elementary Curriculum*. New Delhi: Discovery Publishing House. ISBN 81-7141-845-9.

Ediger, Marlow and Digumarti Bhaskara Rao (2005). *Quality School Education*. New Delhi: Discovery Publishing House. ISBN 81-8356-022-9.

Ediger, Marlow and Digumarti Bhaskara Rao (2006). *Successful School Education*. New Delhi: Discovery Publishing House. ISBN 81-8356-054-7.

Ediger, Marlow and Digumarti Bhaskara Rao (2006). *Successful School Administration*. New Delhi: Discovery Publishing House. ISBN 81-8356-046-6.

Ediger, Marlow and Digumarti Bhaskara Rao (2006). *Issues in School Curruculum*. New Delhi: Discovery Publishing House. ISBN 81-8356-052-0.

Ediger, Marlow and Digumarti Bhaskara Rao (2006). *Community College — Curriculum and Teaching*. New Delhi: Discovery Publishing House. ISBN 81-8356-053-9.

Ediger, Marlow and Digumarti Bhaskara Rao (2006). *Administration of Schools*. New Delhi: Discovery Publishing House. ISBN 81-8356-244-2.

Ediger, Marlow and Digumarti Bhaskara Rao (2006). *Reading Curriculum and Instruction*. New Delhi: Discovery Publishing House. ISBN 81-8356-266-3.

Ediger, Marlow and Digumarti Bhaskara Rao (2006). *Curriculum Organisation*. New Delhi: Discovery Publishing House. ISBN 81-8356-205-1.

Ediger, Marlow and Digumarti Bhaskara Rao (2006). *Curriculum of School Subjects*. New Delhi: Discovery Publishing House. ISBN 81-8356-207-8.

Ediger, Marlow, B.S.V. Dutt and Digumarti Bhaskara Rao (2003). *Teaching English Successfully*. New Delhi: Discovery Publishing House. ISBN 81-7141-707-8.

Ediger, Marlow and Digumarti Bhaskara Rao (2007). *School Science Education*. New Delhi: Discovery Publishing House. ISBN 81-8356-352-X.

Ediger, Marlow and Digumarti Bhaskara Rao (2007). *Language Arts Education*. New Delhi: Discovery Publishing House. ISBN 81-8356-333-3.

Ediger, Marlow and Digumarti Bhaskara Rao (2010). *Effective Schooling*. New Delhi: Discovery Publishing House. ISBN 978-81-8356-613-1.

Ediger, Marlow and Digumarti Bhaskara Rao (2010). *Effective School Curriculum*. New Delhi: Discovery Publishing House. ISBN 978-81-8356-585-1.

Ediger, Marlow and Digumarti Bhaskara Rao (2010). *Essays on Teaching Science*. New Delhi: Discovery Publishing House. ISBN 978-81-8356-882-1.

Ediger, Marlow and Digumarti Bhaskara Rao (2010). *Essays on Teaching Social Studies*. New Delhi: Discovery Publishing House. ISBN 978-81-8356-883-8.

Ediger, Marlow and Digumarti Bhaskara Rao (2010). *Essays on Teaching Reading*. New Delhi: Discovery Publishing House. ISBN 978-81-8356-881-4.

Ediger, Marlow and Digumarti Bhaskara Rao (2010). *Essays on Teaching Mathematics*. New Delhi: Discovery Publishing House. ISBN 978-81-8356-880-7.

Elizabeth, M.E.S., Author and Digumarti Bhaskara Rao, Editor (2004). *Methods of Teaching English*. New Delhi: Discovery Publishing House. ISBN 81-7141-809-0.

Elizabeth, M.E.S., Author and Digumarti Bhaskara Rao, Editor (2004). *Acquisition of English Vocabulary*. New Delhi: Discovery Publishing House. ISBN 81-8356-075-X.

Fatima, Sk. Author and Digumarti Bhaskara Rao, Editor (2007). *Reasoning Ability of School Students*. New Delhi: Discovery Publishing House. ISBN 81-8356-330-9.

Fatima, Sk. and Digumarti Bhaskara Rao (2008). *Reasoning Ability of Adolescent Students*. New Delhi: Discovery Publishing House. ISBN 978-81-8356-315-4.

Gopala Krishna, M., Author and Digumarti Bhaskara Rao, Editor (2007). *Techniques of Teaching Physical Education*. New Delhi: Sonali Publications. ISBN 81-8411-044-8.

Gopala Krishna, M., Author and Digumarti Bhaskara Rao, Editor (2007). *Techniques of Teaching Education*. New Delhi: Sonali Publications. ISBN 81-8411-062-6.

Harshitha, Digumarthi, Author and Digumarti Bhaskara Rao, Editor (2004). *Methods of Teaching Information Technology*. New Delhi: Discovery Publishing House. ISBN 81-7141-805-8.

Harshitha, Digumarthi, Author and Digumarti Bhaskara Rao, Editor (2007). *Techniques of Teaching Computer Science*. New Delhi: Sonali Publications. ISBN 81-8411-036-7.

Indira Devi, Author and J. Prasanth Kumar and Digumarti Bhaskara Rao, Editors (2004). *Values in Language Text Books*. New Delhi: Discovery Publishing House. ISBN 81-7141-833-3.

Jalaja Kumari, C., Author and Digumarti Bhaskara Rao, Editor (2004). *Methods of Teaching Educational Technology*. New Delhi: Discovery Publishing House. ISBN 81-7141-810-4.

Jalaja Kumari, C., Author and Digumarti Bhaskara Rao, Editor (2007). *Job Satisfaction of Teachers*. New Delhi: Discovery Publishing House. ISBN 81-8356-329-5.

Janardhan Reddy, B., Author and Digumarti Bhaskara Rao, Editor (2006). *Techniques of Teaching Sociology*. New Delhi: Sonali Publications. ISBN 81-8411-042-1.

Jayasree, K., Author and Digumarti Bhaskara Rao, Editor (1999). *Correlates of Socialisation*. New Delhi: Discovery Publishing House. ISBN 81-7141-517-2.

Jayasree, K., Author and Digumarti Bhaskara Rao, Editor (2004). *Methods of Teaching Science*. New Delhi: Discovery Publishing House. ISBN 81-7141-801-5.

John Babu, C., Author and T.J.R. Prasad, G.M. Madhukar and Digumarti Bhaskara Rao, Editors (2004). *Problem Solving in Mathematics*. New Delhi: APH Publishing Corporation. ISBN 81-7648-273-0.

Joseph Raju, B and G.A. Anitha, Authors and Digumarti Bhaskara Rao, Editor (2004). *Population Education*. New Delhi: Sonali Publications. ISBN 81-88836-31-3.

Jyosthana, M., Author and Digumarti Bhaskara Rao, Editor (2011). *Achievement Motivation and Achievement in English of School Students*. New Delhi: Discovery Publishing House.

Lalitha, T., Author and K.S. Prabhakaram, D.S.N. Sastry and Digumarti Bhaskara Rao, Editors (2004). *Educational Philosophic Beliefs*. New Delhi: Discovery Publishing House. ISBN 81-7141-765-5.

Krishna, G., Author and Digumarti Bhaskara Rao, Editor (2006). *Techniques of Teaching Physical Education*. New Delhi: Sonali Publications. ISBN 81-8411-044-8.

Kumar Raja, G., Author and Digumarti Bhaskara Rao, Editor (2007). *Principles of Primary School*. New Delhi: Sonali Publications. ISBN 81-8411-054-5.

Lakshmi Kumari, V., Author and Digumarti Bhaskara Rao, Editor (2006). *Techniques of Teaching Home Science*. New Delhi: Sonali Publications. ISBN 81-8411-048-0.

Madhava, K., Author and Digumarti Bhaskara Rao, Editor (2008). *Personality of Adolescent Students*. New Delhi: Discovery Publishing House. ISBN 978-81-8356-262-1.

Madhu Bala, Jampala, Author and Digumarti Bhaskara Rao, Editor (2004). *Methods of Teaching Exceptional Children*. New Delhi: Discovery Publishing House. ISBN 81-7141-802-3.

Mallikarjuna Reddy, V., Author and Digumarti Bhaskara Rao, Editor (2011). *Teaching Aptitude, Social Adjustment and Job Satisfaction of Science Teachers*. New Delhi: Discovery Publishing House.

Marja, Talvi and Digumarti Bhaskara Rao, Editors (1996). *Educational Leadership and Social Changes*. New Delhi: Discovery Publishing House. ISBN 81-7141-320-X.

Naga Kumari, U., Author and Digumarti Bhaskara Rao, Editor (2008). *Science Process Skills of School Students*. New Delhi: Discovery Publishing House. ISBN 978-81-8356-263-8.

Nageswara Rao, S. and M. Srihari, Authors and Digumarti Bhaskara Rao, Editor (2004). *Guidance and Counselling*. New Delhi: Discovery Publishing House. ISBN 81-7141-840-6.

Nageswara Rao, S., Author and Digumarti Bhaskara Rao, Editor (2006). *Techniques of Teaching Psychology*. New Delhi: Sonali Publications. ISBN 81-8411-040-5.

Nageswara Rao, S. and P. Sridhar, Authors and Digumarti Bhaskara Rao, Editor (2004). *Methods and Techniques of Teaching*. New Delhi: Sonali Publications. ISBN 81-88836-33-8.

Nirmala Jyothi, M., Author and Digumarti Bhaskara Rao, Editor (2003). *Non-detention System in School Education*. New Delhi: Discovery Publishing House. ISBN 81-7141-654-3.

Padma Tulasi, G., Author and Digumarti Bhaskara Rao, Editor (2004). *Methods of Teaching Elementary Science*. New Delhi: Discovery Publishing House. ISBN 81-7141-871-6.

Pala Prasada Rao, V., Author and K. N. Rani and D. Bhaskara Rao, Editors (2004). *India Pakistan: Partition Perspectives in Indo English Novels*. New Delhi: Discovery Publishing House. ISBN 81-7141-871-6.

Pala Prasada Rao, V., Author and D. Bhaskara Rao, Editors (2008). *Functioning of Autonomous Colleges*. New Delhi: Sonali Publications. ISBN 978-81-8356-258-4.

Pitchi Reddy, M., Author and Digumarti Bhaskara Rao, Editor (2007). *Techniques of Teaching Social Sciences*. New Delhi: Sonali Publications. ISBN 81-8411-066-X.

Prasad Babu, B., Author and P. Madhu and Digumarti Bhaskara Rao, Editors (2006). *Psychological Adjustment and Well-being*. New Delhi: Discovery Publishing House. ISBN 81-8356-204-3.

Prasad Babu, B., Author and M.V.R. Raju and Digumarti Bhaskara Rao, Editors (2006). *Behavioural Problems of School Children*. New Delhi: Discovery Publishing House. ISBN 81-8356-206-X.

Prabhakaram, K.S., Author and Digumarti Bhaskara Rao, Editors (1998). *Concept Attainment Model in Mathematics Teaching*. New Delhi: Discovery Publishing House. ISBN 81-7141-424-9.

Prasanth Kumar, J., Author and Digumarti Bhaskara Rao, Editor (1998). *Effectiveness of Distance Education System*. New Delhi: Discovery Publishing House. ISBN 81-7141-437-0.

Prasanth Kumar, J., Author and Digumarti Bhaskara Rao, Editor (2004). *Methods of Teaching Civics*. New Delhi: Discovery Publishing House. ISBN 81-7141-806-6.

Prasanth Kumar, J., Author and G. Sundara Rao and Digumarti Bhaskara Rao, Editors (2000). *Open University Student Support Services*. New Delhi: Discovery Publishing House. ISBN 81-7141-550-4.

Raja Kumari, M.A. and D.R.S. Sundari, Authors and Digumarti Bhaskara Rao, Editor (2004). *Special Education*. New Delhi: Discovery Publishing House. ISBN 81-7141-846-5.

Raja Kumari, M.A. and D.R.S. Sundari, Authors and Digumarti Bhaskara Rao, Editor (2004). *Methods of Teaching Educational Psychology*. New Delhi: Discovery Publishing House. ISBN 81-7141-820-1.

Ramatulasamma, K., Author and Digumarti Bhaskara Rao, Editor (2002). *Job Satisfaction of Teacher Educators*. New Delhi: Discovery Publishing House. ISBN 81-7141-655-1.

Rama Krishnaiah, D., Author and Digumarti Bhaskara Rao, Editor (1998). *Job Satisfaction of College Teachers*. New Delhi: Discovery Publishing House. ISBN 81-7141-438-9.

Rama Kumar Ratnam, M.V., Author and Digumarti Bhaskara Rao, Editor (1998). *Dukkha: Suffering in Early Buddhism*. New Delhi: Discovery Publishing House. ISBN 81-7141-653-5.

Rama Krishna Prasad and P. Vide Sagar, Authors and Digumarti Bhaskara Rao, Editor (2004). *Methods of Teaching Physical Education*. New Delhi: Discovery Publishing House. ISBN 81-7141-868-6.

Rama Seshaiah, P. Author and Digumarti Bhaskara Rao, Editor (2004). *Methods of Teaching Home Science*. New Delhi: Discovery Publishing House. ISBN 81-7141-916-X.

Rama Swamy, K., Author and Digumarti Bhaskara Rao, Editor (2007). *Techniques of Teaching Environmental Science.* New Delhi: Sonali Publications. ISBN 81-8411-035-9.

Ramesh, A.R., Author and Digumarti Bhaskara Rao, Editor (2006). *Techniques of Teaching Commerce.* New Delhi: Sonali Publications. ISBN 81-8411-043-X.

Ramesh, Ghanta and Digumarti Bhaskara Rao, Editors (1998). *Environmental Education: Problems and Prospects.* New Delhi: Discovery Publishing House. ISBN 81-7141-423-0.

Ranga Rao, B., Author and Digumarti Bhaskara Rao, Editor (2007). *Techniques of Teaching Economics.* New Delhi: Sonali Publications. ISBN 81-8411-056-1.

Ranga Rao, R., Author and Digumarti Bhaskara Rao, Editor (2004). *Methods of Teacher Teaching.* New Delhi: Discovery Publishing House. ISBN 81-7141-812-0.

Rani, S.S., Author and Digumarti Bhaskara Rao, Editor (2006). *Techniques of Teaching Botany.* New Delhi: Discovery Publishing House. ISBN 81-8411-037-5.

Rathaiah, Lavu and Digumarti Bhaskara Rao, Editors (1996), *International Innovations in Education.* New Delhi: Discovery Publishing House. ISBN 81-7141-359-5.

Rathaiah, Lavu and Digumarti Bhaskara Rao (1997). *Achievement Correlates.* New Delhi: Discovery Publishing House. ISBN 81-7141- 385-4.

Ravi Krishna, M., Author and Digumarti Bhaskara Rao, Editor (2004). *Examination System.* New Delhi: Discovery Publishing House. ISBN 81-7141-824-4.

Ravi Kumar, M., Author and Digumarti Bhaskara Rao, Editor (2004). *Methods of Teaching Computer Science.* New Delhi: Discovery Publishing House. ISBN 81-7141-823-6.

Rudramamba, B., Author and Digumarti Bhaskara Rao, Editor (2003). *Problems of Teaching.* New Delhi: APH Publishing Corporation. ISBN 81-7648-462-8.

Rudramamba, B. and V. Lakshmi Kumari, Authors and Digumarti Bhaskara Rao, Editor (2004). *Methods of Teaching Economics*. New Delhi: Discovery Publishing House. ISBN 81-7141-900-3.

Sambasiva Rao, P., Author and Digumarti Bhaskara Rao, Editor (2007). *Techniques of Teaching Psychology*. New Delhi: Sonali Publications. ISBN 81-8411-040-5.

Sanjeeva Rao, P.C., Author and Digumarti Bhaskara Rao, Editor (1996). *A Text Book of Geology*. New Delhi: Discovery Publishing House. ISBN 81-7141-313-7.

Santhanam, T., B. Prasad Babu and S. Sugandhi, Authors and Digumarti Bhaskara Rao, Editor (2007). *Children with Learning Disabilities*. New Delhi: Sonali Publications. ISBN 81-8411-077-4.

Santhanam, T., B. Prasad Babu and S. Sugandhi, Authors and Digumarti Bhaskara Rao, Editor (2008). *Learning Disabilities and Remedial Programmes*. New Delhi: Discovery Publishing House.

Sarala, M.M.O., Author and Digumarti Bhaskara Rao, Editor (2006). *Techniques of Teaching English*. New Delhi: Sonali Publications. ISBN 81-8411-047-2.

Satya Narayana, G., Author and Digumarti Bhaskara Rao, Editor (2008). *Attitude towards Social Studies and Achievement in Social Studies*. New Delhi: Sonali Publications.

Satya Narayana, V., Author and Digumarti Bhaskara Rao, Editor (2001). *Physical Education, Social Attitudes and Leadership Qualities*. New Delhi: Discovery Publishing House. ISBN 81-7141-593-8.

Satya Narayana, P.V.V. and G. Krishna, Authors and Digumarti Bhaskara Rao, Editor (2004). *Curriculum Development and Management*. New Delhi: Discovery Publishing House. ISBN 81-7141-813-9.

Shamsuddin, Sk. and V. Dayakara Reddy, Authors and Digumarti Bhaskara Rao, Editor (2007). *Academic Achievement and Values*. New Delhi: Discovery Publishing House.

Singh, Y.C., Author and Digumarti Bhaskara Rao, Editor (2006). *Techniques of Teaching Science*. New Delhi: Sonali Publications. ISBN 81-8411-041-3.

Sirisha Rani, S., Author and Digumarti Bhaskara Rao, Editor (2007). *Techniques of Teaching Botany*. New Delhi: Sonali Publications. ISBN 81-8411-037-5.

Sivaratnam Reddy, M., Author and Digumarti Bhaskara Rao, Editor (2004). *Creativity in College Students*. New Delhi: Discovery Publishing House. ISBN 81-7141-697-7.

Siva Lakshmi, G.V. and G.L. Subbaiah, Authors and Digumarti Bhaskara Rao, Editor (2004). *Methods of Teaching Environmental Science*. New Delhi: Discovery Publishing House. ISBN 81-7141-839-2.

Srinivas, G. and Digumarti Bhaskara Rao (2007). *Anxiety of Prospective Teachers*. New Delhi: Sonali Publications. ISBN 81-8411-084-7.

Srinivas, G. and Digumarti Bhaskara Rao (2011). *Intelligence and Personality of Prospective Teachers*. New Delhi: Discovery Publishing House.

Srinivas, M. and I. Prasada Rao, Authors and Digumarti Bhaskara Rao, Editor (2004). *Methods of Teaching History*. New Delhi: Discovery Publishing House. ISBN 81-7141-803-1.

Srinivas Rao, P., Author and Digumarti Bhaskara Rao, Editor (2007). *Principles of Secondary School*. New Delhi: Sonali Publications. ISBN 81-8411-058-8.

Srinivasulu, K., Author and Digumarti Bhaskara Rao, Editor (2011). *Achievement Motivation and Academic Achievement of Alcoholic and Non-alcoholic College Students*. New Delhi: Discovery Publishing House Pvt. Ltd.

Srinivasulu Reddy, M. and K.R.S. Sambasiva Rao, Authors and Digumarti Bhaskara Rao, Editor (1999). *A Text Book of Aquaculture*. New Delhi: Discovery Publishing House. ISBN 81-7141-482-6.

Srinivasa Rao, Mandalapu, Author and Digumarti Bhaskara Rao, Editor (2003). *Achievement Motivation and Achievement in Mathematics*. New Delhi: Discovery Publishing House. ISBN 81-7141-674-8.

Srihari, M., Author and Digumarti Bhaskara Rao, Editor (2003). *Values of Prospective Teachers*. New Delhi: Discovery Publishing House. ISBN 81-8356-328-7.

Subba Rao, K., Author and Digumarti Bhaskara Rao, Editor (2007). *School Education Policy*. New Delhi: Discovery Publishing House. ISBN 81-8356-285-X.

Subba Rao, K., Author and Digumarti Bhaskara Rao, Editor (2007). *Education Planning*. New Delhi: Sonali Publications. ISBN 81-8411-053-7.

Subramanyam, N.R., Author and Digumarti Bhaskara Rao, Editor (2011). *Effectiveness of In-service Training Programmes*. New Delhi: Discovery Publishing House Pvt. Ltd.

Sudhakar Reddy, Y., Author and Digumarti Bhaskara Rao, Editor (2003). *Creativity in Adolescents*. New Delhi: Discovery Publishing House. ISBN 81-7141-659-4.

Sunil Kumar, K. and K. Rama Krishana, Authors and Digumarti Bhaskara Rao, Editor (2004). *Methods of Teaching Chemistry*. New Delhi: Discovery Publishing House. ISBN 81-7141-913-5.

Suneetha, G., Author and Digumarti Bhaskara Rao, Editor (2004). *Environmental Awareness of School Students*. New Delhi: Sonali Publications. ISBN 81-8411-085-5.

Sunita, E. and R. Sambasiva Rao, Authors and Digumarti Bhaskara Rao, Editor (2004). *Methods of Teaching Mathematics*. New Delhi: Discovery Publishing House. ISBN 81-7141-915-1.

Surya Madhava, I., Author and Digumarti Bhaskara Rao, Editor (2006). *Techniques of Teaching Geography*. New Delhi: Sonali Publications. ISBN 81-8411-034-0.

Surya Madhava, I., Author and Digumarti Bhaskara Rao, Editor (2007). *Techniques of Teaching Political Science*. New Delhi: Discovery Publishing House. ISBN 81-8411-061-8.

Swamy, K.R., Author and Digumarti Bhaskara Rao, Editor (2006). *Techniques of Teaching Environmental Science*. New Delhi: Discovery Publishing House. ISBN 81-8411-035-9.

Swarna Jyothi, K., Author and Digumarti Bhaskara Rao, Editor (2007). *Educational Research*. New Delhi: Sonali Publications. ISBN 81-8411-063-4.

Swarna Latha, C.D., and Digumarti Bhaskara Rao, Editors (2006). *Encyclopaedia of Biotechnology*, 5 volumes. New Delhi: Discovery Publishing House. ISBN 81-8356-168-3.

Swarupa Rani, T. and J.R. Priyadarshini, Authors and Digumarti Bhaskara Rao, Editor (2004). *Educational Measurement and Evaluation*. New Delhi: Discovery Publishing House. ISBN 81-7141-859-7.

Vanaja, M., Author and Digumarti Bhaskara Rao, Editor (1999). *Inquiry Training Model*. New Delhi: Discovery Publishing House. ISBN 81-7141-515-6.

Vanaja, M., Author and Digumarti Bhaskara Rao, Editor (2004). *Methods of Teaching Physics*. New Delhi: Discovery Publishing House. ISBN 81-7141-867-8

Valeri V. Koustiouk, Author and Digumarti Bhaskara Rao, Editor (2002). *A Text Book of Cryogenics*. New Delhi: Discovery Publishing House. ISBN 81-7141-642-X.

Vamsi Krishna, V., Author and Digumarti Bhaskara Rao, Editor (2004). *School Psychology*. New Delhi: Discovery Publishing House. ISBN 81-7141-880-5.

Veena Kumari, Balusu and Digumarti Bhaskara Rao (1996). *Operation Black Board*. New Delhi: Discovery Publishing House. ISBN 81-8356-354-6.

Veena Kumari, Balusu, Author and Digumarti Bhaskara Rao, Editor (2004). *Methods of Teaching Social Studies*. New Delhi: Discovery Publishing House. ISBN 81-7141-899-6.

Veena Kumari, Balusu, Author and Digumarti Bhaskara Rao, Editor (2000). *Psycho-Social Correlates of Achievement*. New Delhi: Discovery Publishing House. ISBN 81-7141-547-4.

Venkata Rao, B., Author and Digumarti Bhaskara Rao, Editor (2007). *Techniques of Teaching Chemistry*. New Delhi: Sonali Publications. ISBN 81-8411-057-X.

Venkata Rao, P. and Digumarti Bhaskara Rao (1989). *A Text Book of Zoology — Junior Intermediate*. Guntur: Vignan Publishers.

Venkata Rao, P. and Digumarti Bhaskara Rao (1989). *A Text Book of Zoology — Senior Intermediate*. Guntur: Vignan Publishers.

Venkateswara Rao, V., Author and Digumarti Bhaskara Rao, Editor (2004). *Problems of Education*. New Delhi: Discovery Publishing House. ISBN 81-7141-841-4.

Venkateswara Rao, V., V. Vijaya Lakshmi and V. Vamsi Krishna, Authors and Digumarti Bhaskara Rao, Editor (2004). *Education For All*. New Delhi: Sonali Publications. ISBN 81-88836-30-3.

Venkateswara Rao, V., V. Vijaya Lakshmi and V. Vamsi Krishna, Authors and Digumarti Bhaskara Rao, Editor (2004). *Education in India*. New Delhi: Sonali Publications. ISBN 81-88836-858-9.

Venkateswara Reddy, L. and Narayana, M. L., Authors and Digumarti Bhaskara Rao, Editor (2004). *Education for Dalits*. New Delhi: Discovery Publishing House. ISBN 81-7141-872-4.

Venkateswara Reddy, L. and Narayana, M. L, Authors and Digumarti Bhaskara Rao, Editor (2004). *Methods of Teaching Rural Sociology*. New Delhi: Discovery Publishing House. ISBN 81-7141-811-2.

Venkateswarlu, K. and S.J. Basha, Authors and Digumarti Bhaskara Rao, Editor (2004). *Methods of Teaching Commerce*. New Delhi: Discovery Publishing House. ISBN 81-7141-808-2.

Venugopala Rao, K., Author and Digumarti Bhaskara Rao, Editor (2000). *Teacher Morale in Secondary Schools*. New Delhi: Discovery Publishing House. ISBN 81-7141-551-2.

Venugopala Rao, K., Author and Digumarti Bhaskara Rao, Editor (2007). *Techniques of Teaching History*. New Delhi: Sonali Publications. ISBN 81-8411-059-6.

Vidya, C., Author and Digumarti Bhaskara Rao, Editor (1996). *A Text Book of Nutrition*. New Delhi: Discovery Publishing House. ISBN 81-7141-309-9.

Vimala, T.D., B. Prasad Babu and Digumarti Bhaskara Rao, Editors (2007). *Stress, Coping and Management*. New Delhi: Sonali Publications. ISBN 81-8411-086-3.

Vijaya Bharathi, D., Author and Digumarti Bhaskara Rao, Editor (2000). *Educational Philosophies of Swami Vivekananda and John Dewey*. New Delhi: APH Publishing House. ISBN 81-7648-309-9.

Vijaya Bharathi, D., Author and Digumarti Bhaskara Rao, Editor (2005). *Educational Philosophy of John Dewey*. New Delhi: Discovery Publishing House. ISBN 81-8356-024-5.

Vijaya Bharathi, D., Author and Digumarti Bhaskara Rao, Editor (2005). *Educational Philosophy of Swami Vivekananda*. New Delhi: Discovery Publishing House. ISBN 81-8356-023-7.

Vijaya Lakshmi, D., Author and Digumarti Bhaskara Rao, Editor (2004) *Basic Education*. New Delhi: Discovery Publishing House. ISBN 81-7141-881-3.

Vijaya Lakshmi, V., Author and Digumarti Bhaskara Rao, Editor (2006). *Techniques of Teaching Music*. New Delhi: Sonali Publications. ISBN 81-8411-038-3.

Vijaya Kumar, S.J., Author and Digumarti Bhaskara Rao, Editor (2006). *Techniques of Teaching Mathematics*. New Delhi: Sonali Publications. ISBN 81-8411-039-1.

Visalakshi, V., Author and Digumarti Bhaskara Rao, Editor (2006). *Techniques of Teaching Biology*. New Delhi: Sonali Publications. ISBN 81-8411-045-6.

Visalakshi, V., Author and Digumarti Bhaskara Rao, Editor (2007). *Techniques of Teaching Zoology*. New Delhi: Sonali Publications. ISBN 81-8411-055-3.

Books in Telugu Language

Bhaskara Rao, Digumarti (1986). *Dhrushya Sravana Bodhanapakaranalu* (Audio Visual Teaching Aids). Guntur: Nagarjuna Publishers.

Bhaskara Rao, Digumarti (1993). *Jeevasashtra Bodhana* (Teaching of Biology). Guntur: Nagarjuna Publishers.

Bhaskara Rao, Digumarti (1995). *Vignanasasthra Bodhana* (Teaching of science) Guntur: Nagarjuna Publishers.

Bhaskara Rao, Digumarti (1994). *Vidya Manovignana Sastram* (Educational Psychology). Guntur: Nagarjuna Publishers.

Bhaskara Rao, Digumarti (1997). *Vidya Manovignana Sastram* (Educational Psychology). Guntur: Creative Press.

Bhaskara Rao, Digumarti (1998). *DSC Study Material*. Guntur: Nagarjuna Publishers.

Bhaskara Rao, Digumarti (1998). *Upadhyayudu Vidya*. (Teacher and Education) Guntur: Nagarjuna Publishers.

Bhaskara Rao, Digumarti (1998). *Vidya Drukpadalu* (Perspectives of Education). Guntur: Nagarjuna Publishers.

Bhaskara Rao, Digumarti (1999). *EdCET Teaching Aptitude*. Guntur: Nagarjuna Publishers.

Bhaskara Rao, Digumarti (2001). *Bharata Samajamulo Upadyayudu Vidhya* (Teacher and Education in Emerging Indian Society). Guntur: Sri Nagarjuna Publishers.

Bhaskara Rao, Digumarti (2001). *Bhoutika Sastra Bodhana Padhatulu* (Methods of Teaching Physical Science). Guntur: Sri Nagarjuna Publishers.

Bhaskara Rao, Digumarti (2001). *Jeeva Sastra Bodhana Padhatulu* (Methods of Teaching Biology).Guntur: Sri Nagarjuna Publishers.

Bhaskara Rao, Digumarti (2001). *Vidya Manovignana Sastram* (Educational Psychology). Guntur: Sri Nagarjuna Publishers.

Bhaskara Rao, Digumarti (2003). *Patasala Yajamanyam/Paripalana* (School Management and Administration). Guntur: Sri Nagarjuna Publishers.

Bhaskara Rao, Digumarti and M. Srihari (2009). *Vardamana Bharata Desamulo Vidya* (Education in Emerging India). Guntur: Sri Nagarjuna Publishers.

Bhaskara Rao, Digumarti and B. Prasad Babu (2009). *Vidya Manovignana Sastram* (Educational Psychology). Guntur: Sri Nagarjuna Publishers.

Bhaskara Rao, Digumarti and B. Prasad Babu (2009). *Pradhamika Vidya mariyu Vileena Vidya Dhrukpadhalu* (Perspectives in Primary Education and Inclusive Education). Guntur: Sri Nagarjuna Publishers.

Bhaskara Rao, Digumarti and K. Subba Rao (2009). *Elementary Vidya, Pranalika, Yajamanyam, Upadyaya Kartavyalu* (Elementary Education, Planning, Management and Teacher Functions). Guntur: Sri Nagarjuna Publishers.

Bhaskara Rao, Digumarti and G. Prasanthi (2009). *Samardya Nirmanamu* (Capacity Building). Guntur: Sri Nagarjuna Publishers.

Bhaskara Rao, Digumarti and A. Jagadish (2009). *Vignansastra Bodhana Padhatulu* (Methods of Teaching Science).Guntur: Sri Nagarjuna Publishers.

Bhaskara Rao, Digumarti, Editor (2010). *Vardamana Bharata Desamulo Vidya – Question Bank* (Education in Emerging India). Guntur: Sri Nagarjuna Publishers.

Bhaskara Rao, Digumarti, Editor (2010). *Vidya Manovignana Sastram – Question Bank* (Educational Psychology). Guntur: Sri Nagarjuna Publishers.

Bhaskara Rao, Digumarti, Editor (2010). *Pradhamika Vidya mariyu Vileena Vidya Dhrukpadhalu — Question Bank* (Perspectives in Primary Education and Inclusive Education). Guntur: Sri Nagarjuna Publishers.

Bhaskara Rao, Digumarti, Editor (2010). *Elementary Vidya, Pranalika, Yajamanyam, Upadyaya Kartavyalu — Question Bank* (Elementary Education, Planning, Management and Teacher Functions). Guntur: Sri Nagarjuna Publishers.

Bhaskara Rao, Digumarti, Editor (2010). *Samardya Nirmanamu — Question Bank* (Capacity Building). Guntur: Sri Nagarjuna Publishers.

Bhaskara Rao, Digumarti, Editor (2010). *Ganithasastra Bodhana Padhatulu — Question Bank* (Methods of Teaching Science). Guntur: Sri Nagarjuna Publishers.

Bhaskara Rao, Digumarti, Editor (2010). *Vignansastra Bodhana Padhatulu — Question Bank* (Methods of Teaching Science). Guntur: Sri Nagarjuna Publishers.

Bhaskara Rao, Digumarti, Editor (2010). *Sanghikasastra Bodhana Padhatulu — Question Bank* (Methods of Teaching Social Studies). Guntur: Sri Nagarjuna Publishers.

Bhaskara Rao, Digumarti, Editor (2010). *Telugu Bodhana Padhatulu — Question Bank* (Methods of Teaching Social Studies). Guntur: Sri Nagarjuna Publishers.

Bhaskara Rao, Digumarti, Editor (2010). *Methods of Teaching English — Question Bank*. Guntur: Sri Nagarjuna Publishers.

Bhaskara Rao, Digumarti, N. Saraja, J. Lalitha and V. Mrunalini, Translators (2008). *Vidya–Samajam (Education - Society). Hyderabad*: Dr. B. R. Ambedkar Open University.

Gopala Krishna, G., A. Rama Krishna, K. Subba Rao and Bhaskara Rao, Digumarti (2004). *Jeevasashtra Bodhana*

Padhatulu (Methods of Teaching of Biological Science). Guntur: Sri Nagarjuna Publishers.

Krishna Murthy, V., K.S. Sudheer Reddy and Digumarti Bhaskara Rao (2004). *Vidya Manovignana Sastra Adharalu* (Foundations of Educational Psychology). Guntur: Sri Nagarjuna Publishers.

Lalini, V., V. Dayakara Reddy, M. Srihari and Digumarti Bhaskara Rao (2004). *Vidya Adharalu* (Foundations of Education). Guntur: Sri Nagarjuna Publishers.

Sastry, G.E.P. and G. Satya Narayana, Authors, Bhaskara Rao, Digumarti, Editor (2009). *Sanghikasastra Bodhana Padhatulu* (Methods of Teaching Social Studies).Guntur: Sri Nagarjuna Publishers.

Subba Rao, K.P., P. Ayodhya and Digumarti Bhaskara Rao (2004). *Patasala Yajamanyam — Vidhya Vyavasthalu* (School Management and Systems of Education). Guntur: Sri Nagarjuna Publishers.

Sudhakar, V., B. Ravindra Babu, D.S. Kumar and Digumarti Bhaskara Rao (2004). *Vidya Sanketika Sastram — Computer Vidhya* (Educational Technology and Computer Education). Guntur: Sri Nagarjuna Publishers.

Index

❑❑❑

OOO